FORGOTTEN BIGFOOTS

AROUND THE WORLD

by

Malcolm Smith

Chapters

INTRODUCTION

No doubt all of you have heard of the Yeti or Abominable Snowman of the Himalayas, and the Bigfoot or Sasquatch of North America. But as far back as1961, with the publication of *Abominable Snowmen: Legend Come to Life*, Ivan T. Sanderson alerted us to the fact that legends and reports of similar creatures exist all over the world. (Well, not exactly all over; even he was unaware of the "yowie", the Australian version of the group.)

Comparing the reports, it is clear that they do not all refer to the same species, but all of them are primates ie ape-like creatures which, unlike the known apes, are bipedal. While the existence of such a creature could remain unknown to science in the remote fastness of the Himalayas, it would appear fantastic to most of us that the same could occur in such a worked-over area as North America. Nevertheless, they all possess certain characteristics which might facilitate it.

First of all, unlike other apes and monkeys, they are nocturnal. Many have, of course, been sighted during the day, but it is at night that they are mostly active. Certainly, most of the encounters close to human habitation have occurred at night. Secondly, they are solitary. An extended family of gorillas would hardly be missed by the local human representatives, but one or two gorillas wandering the forest at night might be a different matter. Thirdly, they are shy of humans almost to the point of phobia.

Finally, because they do not officially exist, people who claim to have seen them are not believed. Scientists do not go out looking for them because they do not officially exist. Most zoologists would not even come out to check of a trail of footprints if it were reported to them. If any zoologist did, and wrote a report on his finding, the odds are that no peer reviewed journal would publish it, and the zoologist himself would become a laughing stock among his colleagues. In short, once an animal has somehow avoided being added to the list of discovered species, that very fact will work to make its "unknown" status permanent.

Not only that, but such mystery animals tend to receive whimsical labels by journalists who only half believe in them. Thus, although there is no logical reason why a large, unknown primate might not exist in the little explored regions of the Himalayas, what scientist could take seriously a "snowman", especially an "abominable" one? To do so would be to commit the cardinal scientific sin of jumping on to the bandwagon of the uneducated masses.

Nevertheless, although such matters fail to get raised at official zoological conferences, they not uncommonly form the subject of informal discussions when zoologists meet around the table. The investigation of such animals is known as "cryptozoology", from the Greek *cryptos*, meaning "hidden", and the animals themselves are called "cryptids".

It is not my intention to cover the whole worldwide field of mystery bipedal apes, or ABSMs (abominable snowmen) as Sanderson labelled them. That would require a volume far thicker than this. Rather, it is to introduce to the English speaking public important articles originally published in French or Spanish, with a couple of obscure English ones thrown in for good measure.

If sometimes my translation appears a little stiff, this is because I have favoured accuracy over elegance. Just the same, I do not claim to be a professional translator, as much at home in the foreign as in my own. On the contrary, I freely admit that, at times, I have run up against phrases which are far from clear, and words which do not appear in any available dictionary. Nevertheless, I am confident that the overall purport of the text has been made clear. Considering all the uncertainty involved in cryptozoology, questions about the precise meaning of a foreign term are low on the list of problems.

My translations have been bracketed with introductions and commentaries, but I have ensured that these are always printed in the San Serif font you are now reading, which is quite different to the font used in the actual translations. You should therefore have no problem distinguishing whether I am speaking on my own bat, or channelling an author.

Naturally, an issue arises about copyright. The translations, of course, are mine, but the copyright for the original articles remains with the original authors, most of whom are impossible to contact, and some of whom are dead. Nevertheless, the originals came mostly from non-commercial journals, many of which were obscure even in their own countries. I am reasonably certain that no-one has been disadvantaged by my translation, but if anyone feels they have been, they are welcome to contact me.

Finally, I wish to thank Michel Raynal for forwarding some of the articles to me.

PART I

ASIA

Asia is a big continent, so you should not be surprised to learn that mystery primates (ABSMs)are rumoured to exist in more than one area.

Such is the *yĕrén*, or "wild man" of China, particularly Hubei province, which had been extensively investigated by a team under Prof. Zhou Guoxing of the the Beijing Museum of Natural History. It is only fair to add, however, that after more than thirty years of research, he reluctantly came to the conclusion that the evidence was bogus.

Indochina's *người rừng* were labelled "rock apes" by the GIs who encountered them, but the Vietnamese name means simply "man of the forest", the equivalent of the Malay "orangutan".

The *orang pendek*, or "short man", isolated in pockets of dense forest in Sumatra, has been the subject of numerous searches, and ranks as the ABSM most likely to be discovered soon, while footprints of perhaps a similar primate, the *batutut*, were discovered in Sabah by zoologist, John MacKinnon while researching wild orangutans. On the other hand, the *orang dalam* ("interior man") of the Malay peninsula appears to be something huge.

However, these cryptids are not the subject of this section. Instead, I am concentrating on three areas: the Chitral region of Pakistan, the Caucasus mountains and, to a limited extent, Mongolia. (Yes, I know that the Caucasus is, strictly speaking, in Europe, but for reasons that will become obvious, their ABSMs are more relevant to Asia). The first two are covered by two lengthy dissertations, but in order to understand their point of view, it is necessary to know the background of a couple of important scholars.

The first was the Belgian-French zoologist, Dr. Bernard Heuvelmans (1916 - 2001), the "father of cryptozoology". It was his book, *On the Track of Unknown Animals*, published in French in 1955 and in English in 1958, which essentially inspired the worldwide interest in mystery animals in general. In 1968 he was visiting the U.S. as the guest of Ivan Sanderson, of *Abominable Snowmen* fame, when they heard about the Minnesota Iceman.

A showman by the name of Frank Hansen had been touring various rural fairs exhibiting what appeared to be some sort of apeman preserved in a block of ice. The two zoologists were allowed to examine it, but only through the enveloping ice. Even so, it was possible to detect the stench of decomposing flesh - an important point, because it implies there was actual meat down there.

Both zoologists were impressed, and were convinced it was genuine. Both published descriptions of it in scientific journals in their respective languages. Heuvelmans was so bold as to provide it with a scientific name: *Homo pongoides*, or "apelike man".

After that, things got a lot murkier. The provenance of the Iceman was never made clear. Various stories circulated. Heuvelmans concluded that it had been shot in Vietnam and smuggled into the U.S. in an army body bag, something never asserted by Hansen, as far as I am aware. There was talk of a model having been made. The specimen was allegedly thawed and refrozen. Finally, it disappeared completely.

Although, strictly speaking, it had never been proven to have been a fraud, it was never proved genuine either, so you pays your money and you takes your chances. For what it is worth, my money is on the fraud. But Dr. Heuvelmans never wavered in his belief that it was genuine, and many French cryptozoologists have followed suit. You will see references to *H. pongoides* in the first chapter.

The second scholar was the Soviet historian, Boris Porshnev (1905 - 1972) whom a visiting Soviet zoologist once described to me as a highly educated polymath. When stories of the abominable snowman of the Himalayas were initially bruited in the 1950s, word passed around in the Soviet Union that they had the same thing in their own country, particularly in the Caucasus, and it was Porshnev who took charge of the investigations. Towards the end of his life, he collaborated with Dr. Heuvelmans, and two years after his death a book was published under their joint authorship: *L'Homme de Néandethal est Toujours Vivants* ("Neanderthal Man in Still Alive).

The result was twofold. Firstly, the Russians always refer to their own ABSMs as "snowmen". Secondly, it appears to have become accepted doctrine among French and Russian cryptozoologists that these mystery primates are "relict Neanderthals" ie the last scattered remnants of our sister species, *Homo neanderthalensis*. This is a highly dubious proposition, as I shall explain in a later chapter.

Finally, based on the Latin word for a human being, *homo*, they refer to their field as "hominology", and the animals as "hominids". This is also an unfortunate development, because in zoology, hominids are members of the family, Hominidae, comprising human beings and our fossil relatives, plus the great apes.

Chapter 1

The Yeti of Pakistan

In India a bandicoot is a large rat, in Australia it is a marsupial. Americans call an elk a moose, a red deer an elk, and a bison a buffalo. In Spain and Portugal a *tigre* is a tiger; in Latin America it is a jaguar.

What has this got to do with the issue of this chapter? Simple. Across the length of the Himalayas there are a host of mutually incomprehensible languages, and consequently a host of different names for a legendary giant primate unknown to science. Westerners have adopted one of these words, "yeti" and translated another as "abominable snowman", and use these as catch-all terms for the animal. But how do we know that all these words refer to the same thing, or even that they are used consistently in the same language? We know that Reinhold Messner, for example, has made a good case (*My Quest for the Yeti*, 1998) that a couple of these words refer to the brown bear.

Therefore, we must be grateful for the work of the late Jordi Magraner (1958 - 2002), the Catalan-born French zoologist who so meticulously researched the issue in Chitral, the narrow triangle of Pakistan squeezed between Kashmir and Afghanistan. It is essentially the western end of the Himalayas. During two expeditions into the region, he managed to locate, and question in their own languages, more than two dozen people who had actually seen the mysterious creature, and obtained information on 63 separate characteristics. He continued to make expeditions into the region, where he was eventually murdered in 2002.

Almost thirty years ago, Michel Raynal sent me a 1992 report by M. Magraner entitled, *Recherches sur les Hominides Reliques d'Asie Centrale* ("Research on the Relict Hominids of Central Asia). As it turned out, this was merely a preliminary report. The complete report has since become available on the internet[1]. At 84 pages in length, it is too long to fully translate here, and much of this consists of the protocol of questions which he asked the witnesses, and the pictures of monkeys, apes, and human ancestors which he showed them. However, he did provide extra eye witness accounts. I have therefore chosen to translate the basic descriptions of the environment, plus the testimonies.

. . . .

---

[1] http://daruc.pagesperso-orange.fr/hominidesreliquesasiecentrale.pdf

Scientific Expedition
by
Jordi Magraner
National Museum of Natural History
25 rue Cuvier, 75005 Paris, France

OBJECTIVES

The study has as its objective to characterize on the ground elements to permit verification of the existence of hominids *stricto sensu* through the study of the ecological and human context and the use of a protocol to analyse the testimonies.

In order to arrive at a working basis on which to arrange the study, a questionnaire on the presumed anatomy of these beings was elaborated. The meticulous examination of *Homo pongoides* by Dr. Heuvelmans, constituting the most complete description of the physical characteristics associated with these beings, was therefore retained as a reference tool. Confronting witnesses on the ground with it served to refute or confirm it.

The choice of the study area came down to North Pakistan. The country of origin of *Homo pongoides*, namely Vietnam, was not at this period propitious for an investigation on the ground; likewise the other regions to which hominids are attributed: the former USSR, China, Iran, or Afghanistan. Among the areas supposedly inhabited by hominids, the District of Chitral appeared the most propitious. This region, which constitutes the wildest part of North Pakistan, never having been the object of similar researches, its population would therefore be considered as virgin of all influences from earlier investigations. Furthermore, also known as Little Kashgar, its geographic proximity to Greater Kashgar, which was defined by Dr. B. F. Porshnev as one of the zones most favourable to being a permanent hominid habitat, constituted a supplementary argument.

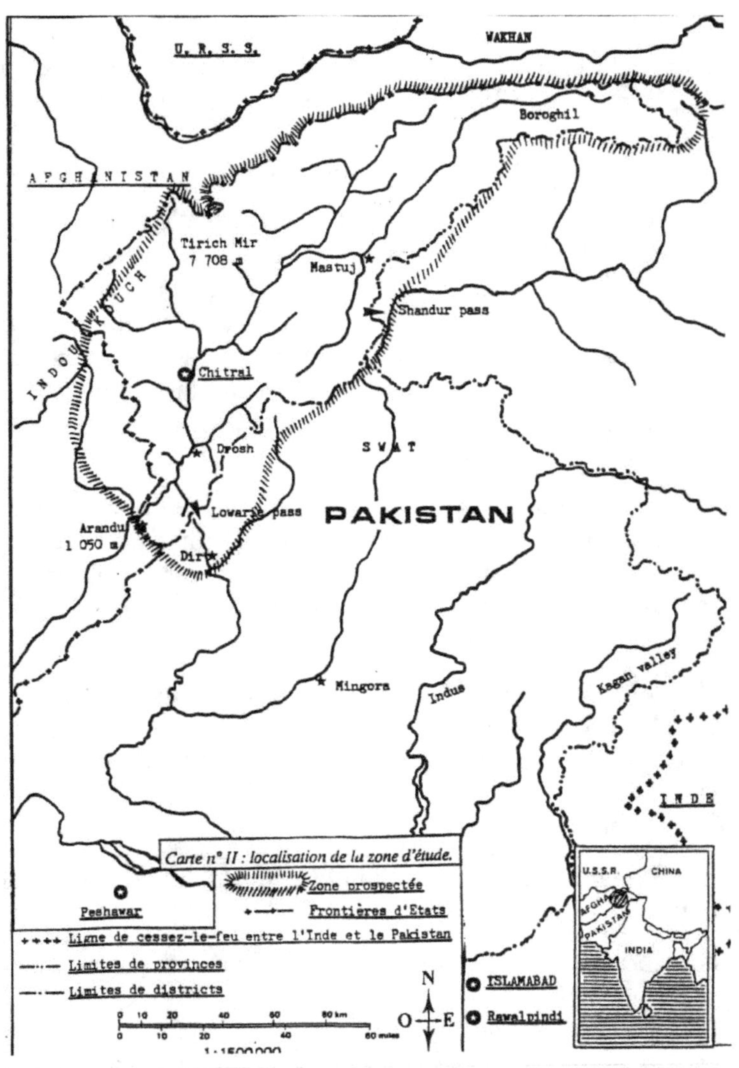

It is simpler to just translate the legend at the bottom. From top to bottom the lines represent:
zone of study
national borders
cease fire line between India and Pakistan
boundaries of provinces
boundaries of districts

. . . .

METHODOLOGY

Two expeditions lasting a total of 19 months were conducted in the District of Chitral, one in 1987-1988, the other in 1990, by a team of two persons.

The methodology utilised was as follows:

- The first step, characterized by the eco-ethnological data which constitute the context of the appearance of the testimonies:
- in order to confront the data furnished by the witnesses and those offered by the natural environment with a view to verifying or refuting the *prima facie* credibility of the existence of hominids.
- The second step, the definition of a protocol for collecting testimonies involving the matrix of several variables:
- the validity of the witnesses:

Two types of informants were retained: the direct observer, who claimed to have observed one of these beings himself, and the direct informer, who gained his information from a direct observer. No testimony obtained by money, or coming from a source more distant than the direct observer was retained.

- the direct transmission of testimonies to the enquirers:

The collection was effected directly in the language of the witness (Khowar or Chitrali) in order to avoid all the deformations inherent in the use of a translator.

- The systematisation of the testimonies:

The testimonies were directly transcribed in the form of a protocol comprising:

- Basic information concerning the observation:

  - observer: name, age, ethnicity, occupation
  - observation: local name, environment, altitude, date, hour
  - distance and duration of the observation
  - what was observed: indices of the animal's presence, or individual(s), sex, age, height
- The witness's spontaneous account repeated several times, without The responses to a questionnaire comprising 63 points relative to the external appearance of the observed beings, and constructed from the characteristics evoked by Dr. Heuvelmans.

- An initial identikit picture produced from the responses and indications given by the witness without intervention by the enquirer.
- The iconographic indicators comprising different species of present day primates (*Homo sapiens*, great apes, local *Macaca mullata*), bears, reconstructions of fossil hominids and primates, as well as three representations of wild hairy men (in the broad sense), from the description described by Dr. Heuvelmans.
- A definitive portrait executed from the iconographic indications chosen by the witness.
- This systematisation permits testing the veracity of the information collected via comparisons within and between testimonies.
- coherence and credibility of the spontaneous descriptions and iconographic representations at the heart of the same testimony.
- coherence and credibility of the testimonies as a whole.

THE NATURAL ENVIRONMENT

It involves the Hindu Kush range. This comprises, in the district of Chitral, 17 summits over 6,000 metres in height over an area of 14,903 km^2.

In the south, at altitude, winter is marked by extremely cold spells (-20°C) and abundant snowfall. In the north, winters are of the continental type: long and dry.

The faunistic and floristic context of the zone under study is listed as being in the Palaearctic Region with some influences of the Oriental Region. Two large assemblages can be distinguished: the south dominated by dry forests of evergreen oak or conifers; the north consisting of steppes typical of Central Asia. The fauna varies according to the ecosystem, this region comprising six ecosystems defined by a set of specific species.

....

The chart on the following page (you will have to turn it around) represents the natural environment. The central line represents the months, and is easy to read. Below that is the average monthly precipitation in millimetres (25.4 mm = 1 inch) in the southern part of the district at Drosh, 1465 metres. (1 metres = 3.28 feet).

Below that is the average temperature in degrees Celsius, also at Drosh. (For those who are interested, 0°C = 32°F and 30°C = 86°F.)

The pyramid in the top half represents the land according to altitude, which is shown on the left in metres.

Black = periods with snow.

Stippled = periods without snow.The number of months affected by snowfall are shown on the vertical blocks at left.

The labelling on the right of the pyramid represents the alteration in vegetation cover from bottom (1050 metres) to top (7,000 metres) from (in order) sagebush steppe, evergreen oak, cedar, fir, birch, alpine meadow, rocks, glaciers, and eternal snow, with the limits of cultivation at 2,700 metres, in the lower fir zone.

Most interesting are the bars at the right, which represent the altitudinal distribution of fauna and of the barmanu.

T =   Himalayan snowcock
Mt =   marmot
C =   musk deer
Me =   Himalayan monal, a type of pheasant
ON =   black bear
LN =   snow leopard
M =   markhor (a type of goat)
B =   barmanu
Tr =   domestic flocks
L =   wolf
U =   urial (a type of wild sheep)
A =   agames (translation unknown)

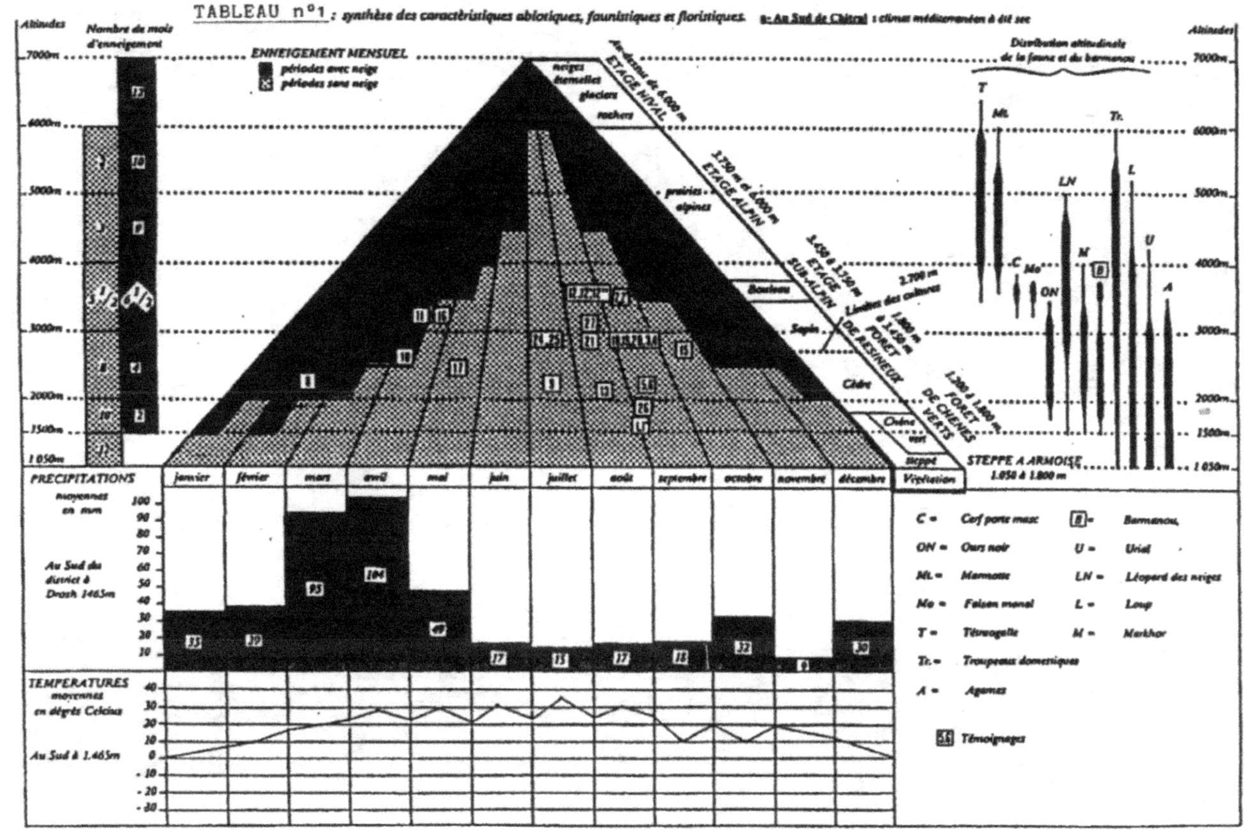

TABLEAU n°1 : synthèse des caractéristiques abiotiques, faunistiques et floristiques.

THE HUMAN CONTEXT

North Pakistan has not known any great civilisations, and is still marked by a social organisation of the feudal kind.

The district of Chitral is characterized by its isolation and absence of infrastructure. Its population is composed of several ethnic groups, such as:

- the Chitralis (the majority): sedentary and living in villages in the valley floors.
- the Gujars: nomadic shepherds situated at the bottom of the social ladder, but occupying the high country.

On the whole, the population is Muslim, with the exception of the polytheistic Kalashs. The very low population density (11 per km^2), which is also concentrated in the valley floors, leaves the upper zones effectively uninhabited.

The geomorphological and ecological context permits the existence of an immense wild zone able to sustain unknown species and favouring the maintenance of isolates. Only the shepherds, and in particular the nomads who live in the high country appear in a position to encounter unknown species or possible wild man populations.

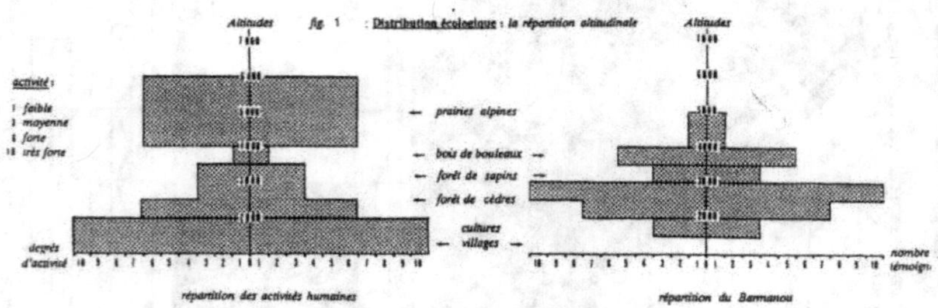

Ecological distribution: altitude and human activity

The horizontal scale of this diagram represents human activity on the left and sightings of the barmanu on the right. The vertical scale represents altitude, with vegetation ranging from villages at the bottom, upwards to cultivated fields ("cultures"), cedar forests ("forêts de cèdres"), fir forests ("forêts de sapins"), birch woodland ("bois de bouleaux"), and finally alpine meadows. It reveals that the forests are the areas where human and barmanu activities overlap and that, contrary to its name, the "abominable snowman" does not live in the snow.

. . . .

THE WITNESSES

We have at our disposal 27 testimonies, of which 21 are from direct observers. A total of 29 people were witnesses to 31 contacts with hairy wild men (24 encounters and 7 observations of tracks) corresponding to 27 individuals.

The probability of encounters increases with human activity in the high country. Indeed, 69% of the witnesses are shepherds. Although 52% of the witnesses are Gujars, it does not prove that ethnic identity constitutes a determining factor.

In the course of the last twenty years, the number of testimonies has increased, undoubtedly due to the massive arrival of nomad Gujar shepherds. Thus, more than 90% of the witnesses relate information collected in the last twenty years, of which 61% is in the last 5 years and 3 testimonies in 1990. The role played by the Gujars together is connected to the way of life as nomad shepherds, and their activities in the high country.

The age of the adult witnesses varies from 24 to 70 years. The name of the wild man varies according to the area:

- *Jangali Mosh* among the Chitralis, which means "forest man" or "wild man".[2]
- *Almasti* more rarely.
- *Barmanu* constitutes the most widespread name in the south. It means "robust", "muscled". Etymologically close to the spoken Hindi *ban manus* (*ban manush*) meaning "forest man", it was perhaps introduced by the Gujars.

---

[2] *Jangal* = our word, "jungle", is the ordinary term in the languages of northern India and Pakistan for wilderness, whether forest or desert. It gained the English meaning of rainforest because the British settled first in Bengal.

GEOGRAPHIC AND ECOLOGICAL DISTRIBUTION OF THE TESTIMONIES

The vast majority of the encounters are situated in the south of the district in the forest belt (26 contacts). They are especially more common in the fir and cedar woods. The altitudinal distribution is located between 1,500 and 4,500 metres with a predominance between 2,000 and 3,000. The encounters are tied to an environment and to a nomadic lifestyle rather than an ethnic identity.

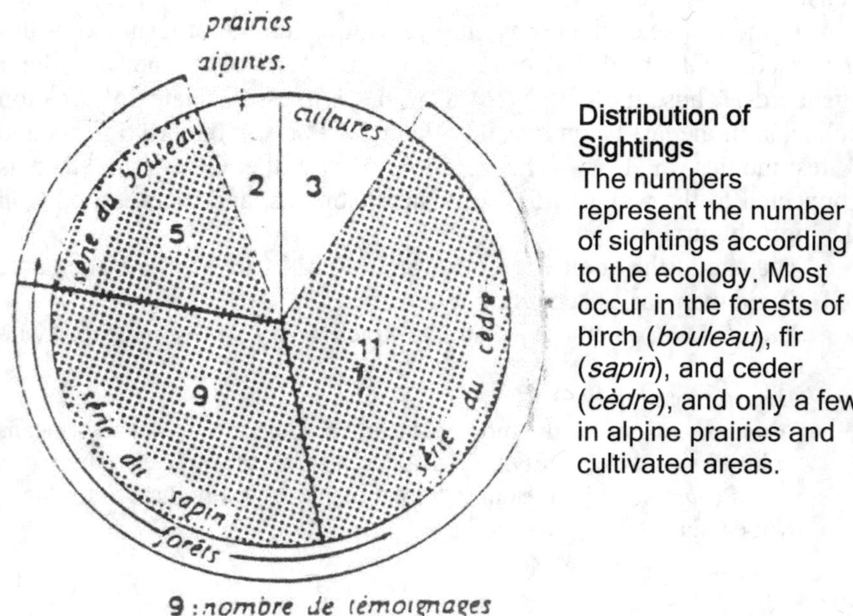

Distribution of Sightings
The numbers represent the number of sightings according to the ecology. Most occur in the forests of birch (*bouleau*), fir (*sapin*), and ceder (*cèdre*), and only a few in alpine prairies and cultivated areas.

THE DISTRIBUTION ACCORDING TO THE CIRCADIAN CYCLE

Comparison of the data permits a coherent synthesis reflecting the rhythm of life of the wild populations. The frequency of testimonies is inversely proportional to human activity. This leads one to the hypothesis of an ethno-ecological separation between the known ethnic groups and the wild populations, with ecological niche sharing in the forest levels according to a circadian shift [i.e. between day and night] .

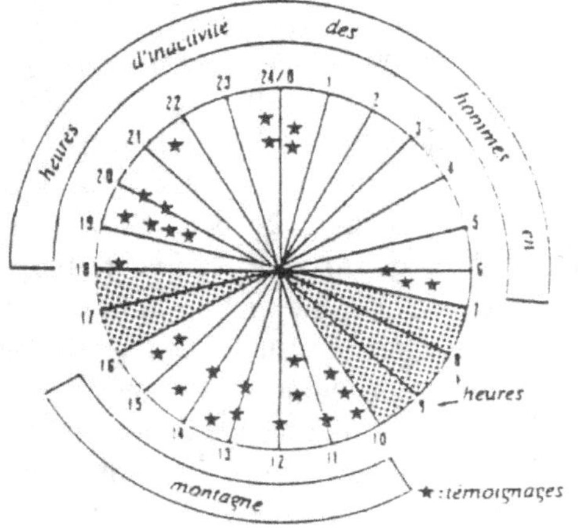

Distribution According to Time of Day
Number of sightings in each hour of the day. The top semi-circle represents the hours of human inactivity, the lower section marked *montagne* when humans are on the mountain side.

THE DISTRIBUTION ACCORDING TO THE ANNUAL CYCLE

The encounters become rare in winter, although the human presence is maintained in the high country, but in a much reduced rhythm. The low probability of encounters may thus be due to the actions of the local populations or to the migratory behaviour of the wild populations.

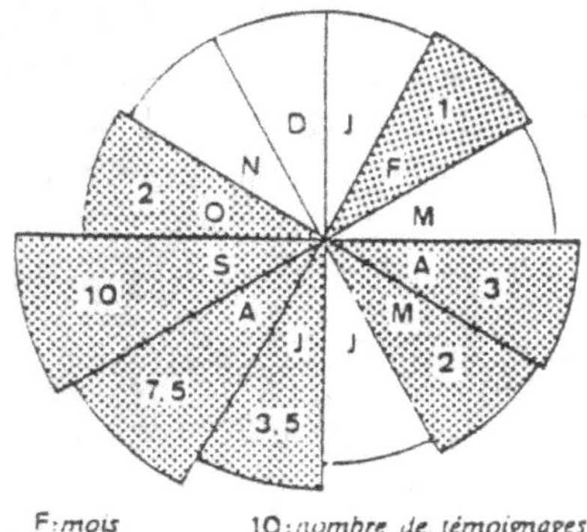

Number of Sightings According to Month

ANATOMIC DESCRIPTIONS

Overall view:

All the physical characteristics collected and the iconographic indications chosen by the witnesses correspond to the specimen described by Heuvelmans.

Systematically the testimonies retain the human appearance, the permanent bipedalism and the abundant hair on the bulk of the body, except for the knees and on the face. The latter is of a dark colour (black, red, brown-grey). The body appears thick-set, massive, and endowed with a strong musculature, with broad shoulders. The height does not differ from that of the locally known ethnic groups, and varied from 1m 70 to 1m 85 [5 ft 7 in to 6 ft 1 in]. The skin is quite visible through the pelage, which is developed rather in length than density. The hair of the head is of variable length: short down to the shoulders, or down to the lower part of the back. The hands and feet present a pelage developed on the upper surface of the body, and comprise the digits. The latter are endowed with narrow, arched nails, especially curved on the feet. The toes are splayed. The length of the foot is within the human variability, but is distinguished by a greater breadth. The feet tend to be oriented towards the median plane (inwards).

The trunk is lengthened, broad, and endowed with a keeled thorax. In the known cases, the breasts of the females descent to the lower belly, and are hairless. The back is, in general, hunched and muscular.

The limbs:

The proportions of the limbs are more difficult to estimate, the data varying as a function of the observer as to the height of the hands. These are described as long and broad. The long, fine thumb, like the other fingers, is situated above the height of the metacarpals. The upper limbs seem long and endowed with forearms which are short in respect to the arms. The lower limbs, crooked or bent, present with shins shorter than the thighs.

The head:

The head is voluminous, elongated, sunken into the shoulders, and endowed with prominent cheekbones. The face is hairless. The nape of the neck is powerful. The nose is turned up, with the nostrils broad and opening forward. There is no labio-nasal fissure. The lower edge of the mandible, especially in males, is delimited by a hairiness with encroaches on the neck and shoulders. The supra-orbital arches are especially projecting, and the eyes are very wide set. The eye-brows are poorly developed and the forehead absent. The mouth, devoid of lips, is wide. The witnesses indicate a well developed chewing mechanism, with teeth of of large size, but nevertheless human (without fangs). The chin is not apparent.

Secondary characteristics:

Sexual dimorphism is not marked. The genital organs are poorly known.

The original preliminary report included these reconstructions of the *barmanu* (left) and Heuvelmans' *Homo pongoides* (right) for comparison.

Finally, the witnesses relate the presence of a disagreeable stench like that of carrion. The voice is powerful, expressed in cries and guttural sounds. No indication of articulated language is reported.[3]

---

[3] Magraner provided further information on the voice in an English article at http://www.bigfootencounters.com/biology/jordi.htm

CONCLUSIONS

The geomorphological, ecological, and human context does not contradict the possibility of the existence of unknown human populations.

The testimonies differ from accounts of a mythical type, which function to provide a cosmological explanation of the universe. The myths are characterized by ample descriptions of the head, detailing the distinctive traits of the mythic personage, and this, in an identical manner in all the discourses emanating from the same ethnic and cultural community.

However, the testimonies collected here draw just a general silhouette typified by its hairiness, its human appearance, its permanent bipedalism, its dark skin, its hunched posture, as well as the disproportion of the different parts of the body compared to the proportions of modern day man.

On the whole, this portrait does not allow an incoherence which contradicts the known data of anthropology of current and fossil species.

THE COLLECTED TESTIMONIES

In the course of the two seasons of enquiry, we collected much information on the relic hominids of Chitral. Within this abundant material we have retained 27 testimonies of encounters, which have served as "specimens" for our study. The encounters permit a certain identification of the creature concerned.

We here present some examples in a narrative style synthetising the report of the observers (spontaneous discourses) and the answers to the questionnaire. The terminology used in French [and English] to define the different anatomic parts in the report are the translations corresponding to the terms or mimes employed by the witnesses to describe these parts, for example: brow ridge = "brru nâl" in Khowar, bent forward = the witness's mime ... The measures given in centimetres correspond to the conversion of English measures used by the witness or to the approximate lengths expressed by gestures. The estimations of measurements are given such as they were transmitted to us, without readjustment on our part. The most technical results are presented in the section, "synthesis on the biology of the relic hominids".

In order to avoid confusion, each time we use the term "man" to designate *Homo sapiens sapiens* we write it with a capital M: Man. We also use the term "hairy man" as a synonym for relic hominid.

We recall that the witnesses have never been contacted by researchers working on this question. They are unedited testimonies.

Important: the drawings representing these hominids are *identikit portraits*. One must not therefore consider them as realistic representations, made from nature, but as reconstructions based on the testimonies and the reference pictures chosen[4]. The body proportions are a function of the duration and distance of observation, as well as the characters which most impressed the witness, for example the shape of the hands, the length of the members etc ... The longer the duration of observation the more realistic is the drawing; in the opposite situation, certain parts which caught the attention of the witness sometimes take on an exaggerated value. Nevertheless, we have preferred to remain faithful to the intentions of the witnesses in reproducing the descriptions given, without correction or interpretation on our part.

Note that not all the testimonies were given in the report.

Testimony No. 2 (See attached sketch.)
Data from Purdum Khan, 52, Chitrali shepherd, collected 25/1/88.

... In September 1977, Purdum Khan was a shepherd watching over his goats towards the summit of the mountain, at an altitude of 3400 – 3500 metres [11,100 to 11,500 ft], sitting on a rock in the middle of a meadow. It was between 15 and 16 hours [3 and 4 o'clock], and the weather was sunny. Suddenly, a stench attracted his attention towards the lower part of the terrain, an odour resembling that of "a dog or a cat which had been run over three days ago", according to his expression. The shepherd then noticed a hairy man, three or four metres below him. He remained there, to observe it for two hours, silently, the hairy man being unable to either see or sense him. The shepherd was not afraid because he had already heard tell of such beings, and he had his axe with him for defence, if need be. Even if it were the first time, it was normal for him to see a hairy man, and it was out of curiosity that he decided to

---

[4] i.e. the set of 73 photos and drawings of modern and prehistoric species, which they presented to the witnesses. They were included as an appendix in the original French document.

observe it. The being in question was a young adult male, of medium height (ie for the region, between 1.70 m and 1.75 m) [5ft 7in to 5ft 9in]. It was sitting "like a Muslim" and was eating ant larvae and nymphs, which it was taking between two fingers, the thumb and index. It was in full sunlight, its musculature and thoracic cage being well developed. The overall appearance was of a man, the body being covered with long hair (8 to 10 cm) [3 to 4 in], of a dark maroon brown in colour. It wasn't wearing any clothing. The hairs on its head were long; its face was broad "like that of a Tajik" (an ethnic group frequently with a Mongoloid head), the cheekbones protruding; it had a sort of beard, and only the cheeks, the nasal area, and around the eyes were hairless. The nose was broad and squashed in "like that of a Chinaman", the nostrils clearly visible. The brow ridges were well developed, broad and prominent, the eyes similar to those of a man, of a dark colour. The ears were of human appearance, but hairy. The forehead was absent and the neck very short. The mouth was big, without apparent lips, with teeth resembling a man's, but more massive. The chin was poorly developed and hairy. The arms and legs were rather long, but more muscular than in a man. In contrast, the hands and feet were very broad, with the palms and soles hairless, and the upper surfaces hairy. The nails, similar to those of a man, on both hands and feet were about two and a half centimetres [one inch] long. To be precise, the fingers were long and the feet very broad in relation to a man's. The penis had an enormous erection, "like a donkey's" (referring, however, to the local donkey, which measures a metre [3 ft 3 in] at the withers). When the hairy man moved on, it walked upright like a man, the thoracic cage in front, the feet turned inwards. The colour of the skin, visible through the hairs, was dark "like that of a Gujar" (an ethnic group with very brown skin). At the approach of a large dog, the hairy man departed straight down the slope, in the direction of the forest.

A few days later, about one in the morning, our witness saw the hairy man a second time, in the same spot. The shepherd was coming down with a young woman; the hairy man took hold of her, the shepherd quickly tore her away from him, the hairy man ran away on seeing the axe Purdun Khan was carrying. The hairy man did not manifest any sign of violence ...[It's a pity they did not interview the young lady.]
Reference picture chosen: The ape man, but with dark skin.[5]

According to our witness, he thinks the relic hominids more or less hibernate and do not reappear until March/April in the mountains. It is rare to see any of them in the winter, but it does happen that they go out in this season to feed, for example on juniper berries. He thinks they are omnivores, but dominantly vegetarian.

It is interesting to note the huge size of the erect penis, then in repose, as other testimonies confirm that it is of small size. It is the first time that this type information has been recorded on the penis of the relic hominids of Asia. It remains to be verified whether if this is a constant characteristic, or whether it is due to a pathological problem[6].

Testimonies Nos. 5 and 7 (See attached sketch.)
Information on footprints and childhood memory of Sar Tor, Gujar goatherd aged 35/40, collected 16/03/88.

---

[5] This was a collection of drawings of body, face, hands, and feet, of a hypothetical creature halfway between an ape and a human.

[6] A pertinent comment. It is not mentioned in any other mystery primates around the world, and is something unlikely to be missed. Even the largest apes, such as the gorilla, have only a spike for a penis in comparison to humans. A man's penis is big because his wife's vagina is wide, due to the fact that it has to accommodate a baby with a large head.

... Our witness, Sar Tor, saw the imprints on the loose soil one day in September 1987, when he was walking in the resinous forest above his home, at 2000/2500 metres [6,500 to 8,200 feet] altitude. The shape of the imprinted foot was similar to a human foot, but with the front part much wider. The length of the print corresponded to a Man of size 43/44 shoe size", that is to say about 26/27 centimetres [10 - 10½ in], for a width "of six inches" or 15 centimetres. The prints were very neat, and allowed the sign of the hair on the top of the foot to appear all around. The trail was heading towards the top of the mountain, every now and then indicating that the hairy man was using its hands to climb up the slope, the prints of these being visible on the spot. They were also of human appearance, being very broad and giving the impression of short, but fine fingers. When the witness said Man, or of human appearance, he was referring to the Gujars, who possess long, narrow hands, with relatively fine fingers in comparison to their size. It did not turn up any marks of hair, neither around nor on the palms of the hands, no more than on the soles of the feet, nor prints of claws …

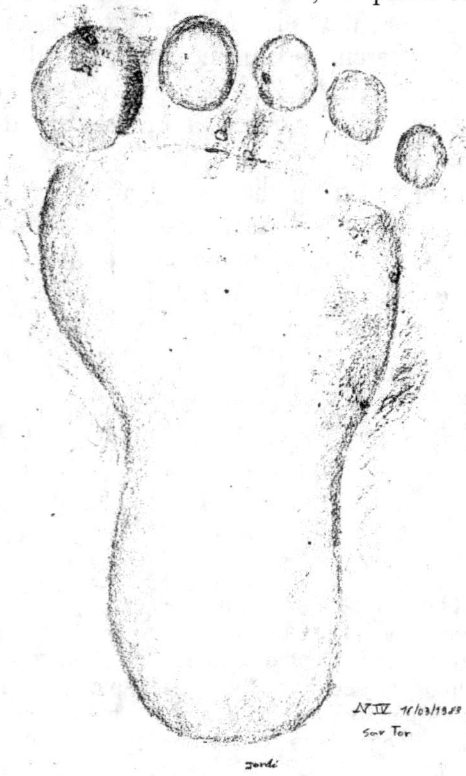

...The goatherd himself had never seen a hairy man, but he retains the description from his grandfather. Sar Tor was young at the time, and was listening ... According to the grandfather, the general demeanour of a hairy man is that of a Man, but the body is entirely covered with light tawny hair. The face is hairless, and from the bottom of the face down to the neck there is a sort of beard. The hair of the head hangs down to the shoulders. The nose is not apparent. It is, as if were, crushed; you cannot see the nostrils. The ears are bigger than a Man's. The eyebrows are not visible, as the hair of the head falls down in front.

The eye lashes are long, but the witness did not remember the description of the eyes. The teeth are big, and protrude, without fangs. The body is squat, the chest broad, the neck thick and short. The height is the same as a Man's, ie between 1.70 m and 1.80 m [5ft 7 in to 5ft 11 in], for the Gujars are rather tall. The feet and hands are broad, the nails, similar to those of a Man, are long and recurved downwards. The hairy men live in the caves in the mountain and feed on roots, and the carcasses of goats and sheep. They are nocturnal but also go out during the day. They seek out Human women[7].

Reference picture: not presented, as he was not a witness to an encounter.

Testimony No. 9 (See attached sketch.)
Information from Mohamad Nabi, Pathan goatherd aged 55, collected 10/04/88.

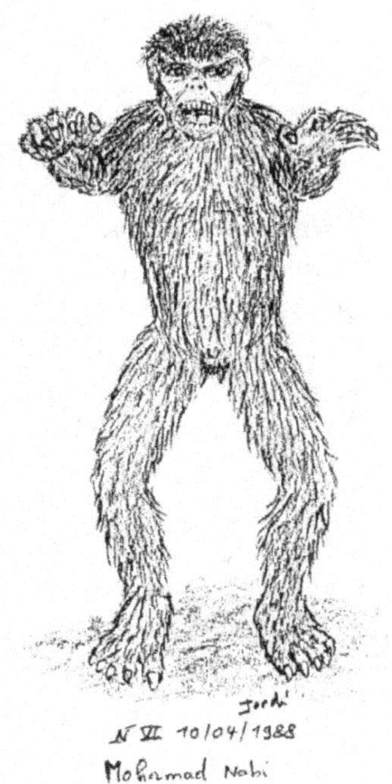

... It was an evening in July 1987, towards 21 hours. The shepherd was returning with his goats towards the village, a lantern in his hand. Suddenly, he fell nose to nose with an adolescent hairy man. The latter then tried to touch Mohamad Nabi by extending its hands (in a defensive posture, not one of real aggression). The goatherd defended himself by striking the hairy youth with his staff. The two protagonists were on a slope planted with bushes and scattered trees, at an altitude of about 2300 metres [7,500 feet]. The two of them were separated by a big bush and were turning around. According to the Pathan, the action lasted about two hours, with him striking the hairy youth and the latter attempting to grab hold of him. The hairy youth was emitting guttural sounds, a form of deep breathing, a sort of groan. The shepherd was not afraid of its bite, but rather of the blows from its hands, these latter having long

---

[7] Note the height mentioned is consistent with the size of the footprints seen, using a body-to-foot ratio of 6.6, which is a useful predictor of human height, within a few inches.

nails which the hairy youth was seeking to use. Its odour was very disagreeable and strong, like that of carrion. It measured 1.10/1.20 metres [3 ft 9 to 3 ft 11 in] in height, and was entirely covered with grey-brown hair.[8] The hair of the head was short; the face, the palms of the hand and the sole of the feet were glabrous. The skin had a dark colour, "like that of a Gujar". It wore no clothes. The forehead was absent, the nose small and crushed, the mouth did not have lips[9], the teeth were similar to those of a Man, without fangs. The arms appeared long to him, because of the hands and their slender fingers. The feet were human in shape but wider, especially the front part. The chest was well developed. At the end of two hours, the hairy youth ran away towards the forest situated above them. The goatherd stipulated that, during both the fight and the flight, the hairy youth was standing fully upright on is legs...
Reference picture chosen: The ape man, but bearing in mind that he was dealing with a young one, that it had short head hair and a dark skin.

Testimonies Nos. 10 and 11 (See attached sketch.)
Information from Mohamad Nabi, the preceding witness, collected 10/04/88.
... Some days before our arrival on the site, this same goatherd, who had fought with a hairy youth, twice saw the trail of a hairy man on different mountains, one of which was just opposite our camp. On 3 April 1988, the trail was crossing a ridge, between 2,500 and 2,600 metres [8,200 to 8,500 feet] in altitude, and seemed to be climbing the valley towards the summit of the mountain. The prints appeared quite recent. On 8 April, the hairy man come from up on the mountain towards 3,500 metres [11,500 feet] altitude.The trail was crossing a valley and setting out again into the rocky escarpments where the markhors [wild goats] live, towards 3,000 metres [10,000 feet] altitude. The prints were a week old, according to our witness, but they were easily visible.
In both cases it involved an adult hairy man, quite big judging from the size of the footprints; perhaps of the same individual. The tracks on both trails were identical in shape and proportions. The foot was long like that of a Man of shoe size 44/45, about 30 centimetres, [12 inches,

---

[8] We must assume that he was wielding the staff with one hand while grasping the lantern with the other.
[9] Everted lips are a human characteristic, absent in all other primates.

equivalent to a height of 6½ feet] but very broad in front. The toes were easily visible, the big toe very clear. There were no marks of claws.

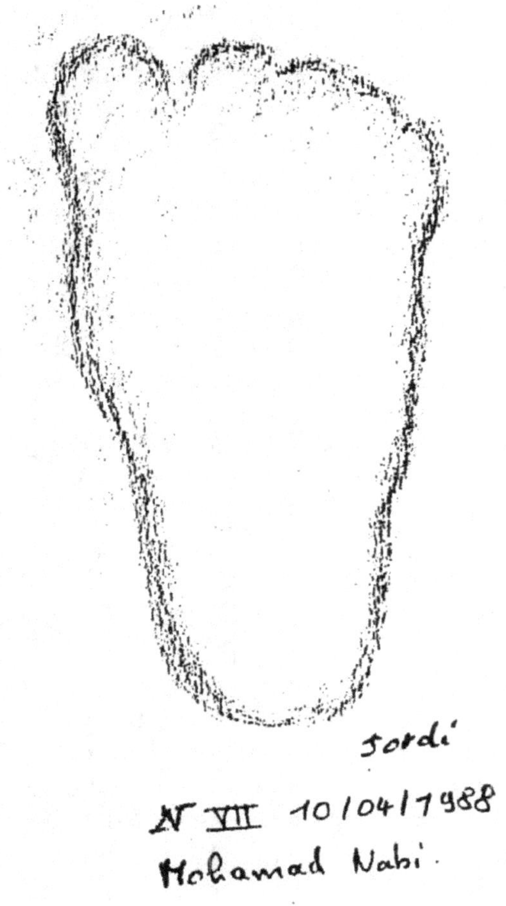

(We located, using a spy-glass and with the aid of the goatherd, the trail of 8 April, which was opposite our camp. One could clearly see the trail of a biped. The tracks came from the east, from up the mountain, crossing a valley and setting out again in the north in the rocky escarpments where it was impossible for a Man to resort without special equipment. The slope was very steep, the rocks very friable, the snow very thick (several metres in places). Considering the characteristics of this trail, it is unthinkable that it could have been made by a native. None of them would have ventured by day over such a terrain, without any foot covering. I have had the experience; in order to move about in such thickness of snow without sinking up to the waist or without leaving in an avalanche, it is necessary to progress by night, when the snow is frozen and stable. It was at that moment that the hairy man moved over the slopes; he alone was capable of going barefooted and in the depth of night in these dangerous zones. A single end of the trail was accessible, in a resinous forest, there where Nabi had seen the footprints clearly, and where the snow was not very deep. Alas for us, the avalanches, the fog and the rain did not permit us to go there until two days later. The tracks were no longer very visible and we were only able to confirm that they involved tracks of a biped on relatively important feet. On the contrary, with the spy-glass, at 60 times enlargement, we were able to analyse the behaviour of the hairy man. We followed its long and prudent detours in order to avoid the cabins occupied by the woodcutters. Its walk did not appear to be rapid and its strides was quite short in relation to the footprints, even in shallow snow. On the descent, it had a tendency to walk diagonally, rarely directly in the direction of the slope. On the high parts, heavily covered in snow, it gave itself up to several slides on its buttocks, on steep but short declines. In the direction of the ascent, on the opposite side, it climbed more or less parallel to the slope. There, where was snow was thick and slope important, it used it hands like oars. Some days later, we were able to observe a new trail, quite high on the mountain, similar to the first. On our part, we were unfortunately confined to our camp by the very changeable climatic conditions, which rendered the mountain dangerous. The warm weather and rain during the day precipitated numerous avalanches ...)

Testimony No. 12 (See attached sketch.)
Data from Lal Khan, Gujar shepherd, aged 55, collected 22/04/88 and completed 30/01/90.

....Our witness has seen a hairy man three times, in August 1985, 1986 and 1987. In 1987, Lal Khan led out his goats to pasture. Towards 1300 hours, he was driving them across a slope opening out onto a meadow at 3450 metres [11,300 ft] altitude. Some goats, by coughing, awoke a hairy man who was lying at the foot of a large spruce. The tree, backed up against some rocks, formed a shelter with the lower branches descending to the ground. The shepherd saw the hairy man leave his shelter. Somewhat frightened at seeing the man, the being in question threw a stone at him, then turned on his heels and calmly crossed the meadow with the aid of a stick held in his left hand. It headed towards the summit and disappeared under a crest. The hairy man halted from time to time in its walk to gather vegetables and eat them. It made a long detour to follow the contours of the ground. The observation lasted more than ten minutes; the frightened shepherd gathered together his goats and made them go back down.

In 1985 and 1986 the witness noticed the same individual in this same area but at a greater distance. At each encounter the same scenario occurred: the shepherd noticed the hairy man, who moved away slowly with the aid of a stick, while he himself being scared, took his goats back down.

In 1987, it was the first time that he saw it so close (10 yards) and that the hairy man threw a stone at him.

The witness described it as like a strong, very hairy man; a heavy pelage over the whole of the body, except for the cheek bones, the palms of the hand, the knees and the ears. It had a beard, short hair on the head, very broad shoulders, and massive teeth, without fangs. The body hair was dark except on the chest, where it was white…

Several details lead one to think that he could have been dealing with an old individual: the slow flight, the aid of a staff, and those white hairs on its chest.

Reference picture: *Homo pongoides*, but with dark skin and short head hair.

Testimony no. 16 (See attached sketch.)
Information from Nur Hamid, Gujar goatherd aged 55, collected on 16/02/90.

One day in April 1987, towards midday, when the sun was veiled, the witness was picking morels [a type of mushroom] with his sister on the mountain, in a coniferous forest situated about 3,000 metres [10,000 ft] altitude. Suddenly, they saw a hairy man. It was 20 metres from them, hunched over in the middle of a bush, in a fetal position (mimed by the shepherd). When it saw them, the being headed towards them. The shepherd and his sister began to throw stones at it and shout. A second man ran over to help them. Finally, the hairy man was touched on the head by a stone, and fled very rapidly. "It ran as fast as a dog." It disappeared into the forest, downhill. The hairy man was tall; it would have measured 1.75/1.80 metres [5ft 9 in - 5 ft 11 in]. The dark skin of its body was completely covered with reddish hair. The long, tangled head of the head hung down to its shoulders. Its imposing musculature and its carriage gave it a squat aspect. Its naked face bore a wide, turned-up nose, it big mouth revealed broad teeth of a human type, without fangs . . .

Reference picture chosen: the ape-man, but with dark skin and thicker eyebrows.

It is interesting to note, as with other reports, it was the presence of the woman which attracted the hairy man. In the presence of Men alone, it always immediately takes to flight.[10]

Testimonies nos. 18, 19, and 20
Information from Mir Mohamad Khan, 30 years, Chitrali peasant-pastoralist, collected 01/04/90.

In September 1989, the witness, who was leading his goats out to graze, saw tracks crossing a coniferous forest at about 3,000 metres [10,000 ft] altitude. It was fine weather and in the afternoon. The tracks resembled those of a Man in their presentation, 26 to 27 centimetres long [10 to 10½ inches, consistent with a height of 5 ft 6 to 5 ft 9] and very broad, about 16 centimetres [6¼ in]. The tracks came from the snow-covered peak of the mountain (the trail was visible from afar) and they were imprinted into the moist earth. This was the third time the goatherd had seen tracks. He was able to observe them in September 1987 and 1988, on dry ground, not far from the same spot, in the same general direction of the trail. The toes of the feet were well separated, and they did not show any lines [uncertain translation], a little as if they were hooked. It did not have any trace of claws. The heel was similar to that of a human. In each case, the strides were long.

It is possible, bearing in mind the resemblance of the trails over three years, their morphological, topographic, and temporal similarities, that they represented three passages by the same individual. [He also illustrated it with *exactly* the same drawing as for testimonies 5 and 7, even down to the inscription at the bottom.]

Testimony No. 22 (See attached sketch.)

Data from Ata ul Llah, 6 and Abdul Hafiz, 14, Chitralis, collected 01/06/90.

... On 24 May 1990 towards 10.30 in the morning, three children, two boys and a girl, were playing close to a canal bordering the village situated at about 2,000 metres [c 6,500 ft] of altitude. It was fine. The girl was the first to see a hairy woman; scared, she hid behind a rock. The

---

[10] [Testimony no. 9 would tend to refute that.]

N. XVII - 01/06/1990

two boys noticed the presence of the hairy woman when she was already at their level. She was coming from the mountain. She headed towards the younger of the boys, threw him to the ground with a blow of her hand, and then seized him. The other boy, terrified, went down towards the village and rejoined the girl. They saw the hairy woman flee towards the mountain with the little boy, aged four years and named Gul Naz. The other two children, terrified and not knowing who this character was, did not dare to say anything at first. The boy did not return home, and sought refuge in a neighbouring garden. His father, towards midday, not seeing them return, began a search and finished by finding him cowering in the garden, still under the influence of fear. The father questioned him and the child began to recount the story. The parents alerted the village.

Footprints of a great size where found close to the canal. At first, after the descriptions of the boy, who said that the stranger had dark skin, the villagers thought that it was a Gujar nomad. A beat of a thousand odd people was organized in the mountain. In vain; they found neither Gujar nor missing child. They concluded that it had been a "Pâri" (spirit) who had carried off the child. Three days later, a group of men located with binoculars some blue clothing at the foot of the rocks. One of them went up and found the missing boy, dead on a rock. Death had been recent, dating about half an hour beforehand; blood was flowing from a hole in the left temple and from another on the left cheek. The child was wearing only his shirt; the shoes and pants had disappeared. The body bore no trace of any other wounds or of ill treatment. They buried him, and the matter was sorted out: it had been the work of a spirit, there was nothing more to be done. The villagers did not even alert the police who, in any case, would not have come out over the death of a young child. To our surprise, they gave us the following explanation: in a society where infant mortality is significant, the death of a child, furthermore one killed by a spirit, is accepted with resignation. The closest police station is many kilometres away, and no-one, in a period of agricultural work, would have accepted wasting time in a useless enquiry, because of the spirit. Indeed, when we had separately interrogated the child witnesses, the boy, then the girl, it became quite clear that it was treated as nothing more than a spirit, in the proper sense of the term. The girl, who was older than the boy, and had a better view of the scene, gave us a very interesting description with the aid of her childish vocabulary.

The being in question was 1.65 to 1.70 metres [5ft 5 in to 5 ft 7 in] in height. Its skin and the long hair of its head were dark. It wore a "big coat" and "big boots" of hair like that of a goat (the district possesses a long haired breed), also dark coloured. The face was large and frightening. Then she added that it turned out to be a woman because she had two enormous breasts which came out of the "coat". It seemed curious to us that someone would walk around under the June sun in a fur coat and boots. Furthermore, nobody here possesses a similar outfit, even for winter. It was quite clear that the little girl, with these words, was describing the pelage of a hairy man. The answers of children to the questionnaire serve to confirm the identity of the being in question ...

... as for the footprints, two or three days before our arrival, it had rained, and the imprints had been wiped out. The descriptions made by the villagers mentioned a foot 23 to 25 centimetres [9 to 10 in] long by 12 to 14 centimetres [4.7 to 5.5 in] wide. These proportions are compatible with the height of the hairy woman.

Reference picture: separately, the two children instantly chose the *Homo pongoides*, in signalling the presence of breasts and the dark colour of the skin.

In regard to the story itself, it is not easy to find reasons which possessed the hairy woman to act like that. Personally, I lean towards the following explanation: the hairy woman had no doubt just lost her own child and, desperate, had been attracted by the cries of the children playing; her maternal instinct set itself on one of them; she kidnapped the smallest one and carried it off as a replacement of her own. The child, at the end of a certain period, succeeded in getting away or was abandoned for one reason or another by the hairy woman. In seeking to regain the village by crossing the rocks, the young boy had a fatal fall. I think that it is less probable that the hairy woman killed him, bearing in mind the circumstances of the discovery of the body. This point of view is shared by the villagers themselves, who recognized that the mortal wounds on the child were caused by a fall. This case of maternal instinct is neither novel nor exceptional; we have numerous examples of it among animals, wild or domestic. It is therefore possible that it would turn up in a being quite close to us (as is a hairy woman).

. . . .

Tables

The author included a table of 27 testimonies - some of them mere footprints - against 63 characteristics, all on a single A4 sized page. The format of this book makes this impossible, so the original table has been converted to several tables. On the next two pages the 63 characteristics are listed. The next two pages record characteristics 1-29 for testimonies 1-13 and 14-26 respectively. (As testimony no. 27 was a footprint, it was not relevant for these characteristics.) The following two pages list the same testimonies against the remainder of the characteristics.

Finally, a synthesis is provided. The data are presented in two sets of columns. From left to right in each set the numbers refer to the characteristic, the number recorded, the percentage, and its presence in males, females, and young.

The author also listed the characteristics against the barmanu, "*Homo pongoides*", and Neanderthal man, but I have not included it. In any case, resemblances are likely to be due simply to a common ancestry.

1.   Abundant hair over the whole of the body
2.   Skin visible through the hair (as with the apes)
3.   Face bare (without beard or moustache)
4.   Eye brows little in evidence
5.   Little hairs scattered over the face
6.   Hair longer on the top of the head (a head of hair)
7.   Hair reduced on the knees
8.   Hair a dark colour
9.   Massive head with the face well developed
10. Head lengthened anterio-posteriorly
11. Very receding forehead
12. Very prominent brow ridges
13. Eyes much separated
14. Dark or brown eyes
15. Cheek bones greatly projecting laterally
16. Pointed ears
17. Elongated ear lobe
18. Nose extremely broad
19. Nose extremely turned up
20. Large nostrils opening towards the front
21. Absence of a groove between the nose and lip
22. Mouth widely split
23. Absence of lips
24. Teeth extremely wide and powerful
25. Prominent jaws forming a flat muzzle
26. Lower jaw narrow, rounded, and massive
27. Chin reduced or absent
28. Posture bent forward (like a crouching ape)
     (a) Seated
     (b) Erect when stopped
     (c) Walking/running on the level
     (d) Walking/running when going down
     (e) Walking/running when going up
     (f) Walking/running horizontally on a slope
     (g) Standing in a posture of observation or defence
29. Head sunken into the shoulders
30. Nape of the neck powerfully developed
31. Back extremely stooped
32. Shoulders extremely wide

33. Thorax quasi-cylindrical with a keeled chest
34. Trunk very elongated
35. Upper limbs long
36. Forearms short in relation to the arms
37. Extremely large hand
38. Hand rather wide
39. Fingers very long
40. Thumb long, slender, and divergent
41. Thumb weakly opposable
42. Finger nails narrow and arched
43. Lower limbs short
44. Bow-legged or bent-kneed
45. Calf short in relation to the thigh
46. Foot short
47. Foot extremely broad
48. Toes fanned out (axis passing between toes II and III)
49. Toes hooked
50. Big toe quite divergent
51. Toes of nearly equal size
52. Little toes curled inwards
53. Toenails narrow and arched
54. Feet turned inwards
55. Hairy goitre or sort of beard
56. Absence of fangs
57. Human appearance
58. Bipedal
59. Long breasts
60. Colour of hair: black, brown, red, dark, light, grey, beige
61. Odour: strong, weak, disagreeable, non-existent, not particular
62. Length of penis: long & slack, small & slack, long &erect, small &
    erect
63. Length of eye-lashes: long, small
    - sex of individual: male, female, young
    - age of individual: adult, young
    - height (individual in metres) or dimensions (prints), length, width in
    cm

Testimonies

	1	2	3	4	5	6	7	8	9	10	11	12	13
1	+	+	+	+		+	+	+	+			+	+
2		+			F				+	F	F	+	
3		+	+	+		+	+	+	+			+	
4		+			O				+	O	O	-	
5												?	
6	+	+	+	+	O	+	+	+	+	O	O	+	+
7		+							+			+	
8		+	+	+	T	+		+	+	T	T	+	+
9		+	+	+				+	+			+	+
10		+			P			+	?	P	P	+	
11		+						+	+			+	
12		+			R			+	+	R	R	+	
13		+						+	+			+	
14		+			I				+	I	I	+	
15		+						+	+			?	
16		-			N					N	N	+	
17		+					+					-	
18		+			T			+	-	T	T	+	
19		+					+	+	+			+	
20		+			S		+	+	+	S	T	+	
21		+							+			+	
22		+						+	+			+	
23		+						+	+			+	
24		+					+		+			+	
25		+						+	+			+	
26		+						+	+			+	
27		+						+	+			+	
28		±	±	-				-	-			-	+
a		+	+										
b													+
c													
d		-	-										
e								-	-			-	
f													
g										-		-	
29		+	+	+			+	+	+			-	+

	14	15	16	17	18	19	20	21	22	23	24	25	26
1	+	+	+	+				+	+	+	+	+	+
2			+		F	F	F	+	+	+	+	+	+
3		+	+	+					+	+	+	+	+
4			-		O	O	O		+				+
5													+
6	+	+	+	+	O	O	O	+	+	+	+	+	+
7									+	+		+	
8	+	+	+	+	T	T	T	-	+	+	+	+	
9	+	+	+	+					+	+	+	+	+
10			+	+	P	P	P	+		+	+	+	
11									+	+	+	+	
12				+	R	R	R		+	+		+	
13				+					+	+		+	+
14					I	I	I		+	+	+	+	
15				+					+	?	+	-	
16					N	N	N	+		+		-	-
17										+			
18				+	T	T	T		+	+	+	+	+
19				+					+	?	+	+	+
20				+	S	S	S		+	?	+	+	+
21													
22									+	+	+	+	+
23									+		+	+	
24										+		+	
25				+					+	+		+	
26				+					+	+		+	
27									+	+		+	
28	+	+	+	-				+	+	+	+	+	-
a													
b		+	+								+		
c	+								+	+			
d			+	-									
e													
f													
g													
29	+	+	+	+				+	+	+	+	+	+

	1	2	3	4	5	6	7	8	9	10	11	12	13
30		+	+	+			+	+	+			+	+
31		±	?	?					?			-	+
32	+	+	+	+				+	?			+	+
33		+	+	+			+	+	+			+	+
34		+	+	+				+	+			-	
35		+	+	+				+	+			+	+
36		+										+	
37		+			+			+	+			+	+
38		+			+		+	+	+			+	+
39		+			+			+	+			+	+
40		+			+				+			+	
41		+										+	
42		+					+		+			+	
43		?	+	+				?	+			?	
44		+	+	+				?	+			+	+
45		+							+			+	
46		+			+			+	+	+	+	+	
47		+	+	+	+		+	+	+	+	+	+	+
48		+			+				+	+	+		
49		+							+				
50		+			+				+	+	+		
51		+			+				+	+	+		
52													
53		+					+		+				
54		+	+	+					+			+	+
55		+	+	+				+	-			+	
56		+							+			+	
57	+	+	+	+	+	+	+	+	+	+	+	+	+
58	+	+	+	+	+	+	+	+	+	+	+	+	+
59	-	-	-	-			-	-	-			-	+
60	d	d.br	r.bl	r.bl		d	be.c	br.g	br.g			d	d
61		s.d							s.d				
62		l.e						sm	sm			sm	
63							L						
	M	M	M	M	?	M	M	M	M	?	?	M	F
	A	A	A	A	A	A	A	A	Y	A	A	A	A
	1.7	1.7- 1.75	1.7	1.7	26.5 15	1.7 5 1.8	1.7 1.8	1.7	1.1 1.2	30 19	30 20	1.7 1.75	1.7

	14	15	16	17	18	19	20	21	22	23	24	25	26	27
30	+	+	+						+	+	+	+	+	
31	+	+	+		F	F	F	+	+	+	+	+	-	F
32	+	+	+	+	O	O	O	+	+	+	+	+	+	O
33	+	+	+	+	O	O	O	+	+	+	+	+	+	O
34	+	+	+	+	T	T	T	+	+	?	+	+	+	T
35	+	+	+	+	P	P	P	+	+	+	?	+	+	P
36			+	+	R	R	R				+	+	+	R
37		+	+	+	I	I	I	+	+	+	?	+	+	I
38		+	+	+	N	N	N	+	+	+	?	+	+	N
39		+	+	+	T	T	T	+	+	+	+	+	+	T
40			+	+	S	S	S			+			?	S
41														
42												+	+	
43		+	+	-					+	+	+	?	-	
44	+	+	+	+				+	+	+	+	+	-	
45										+	+	+	+	
46			+		+	+	+	+	+	+	+	+	+	+
47	+	+	+	+	+	+	+	+	+	+	?	-	+	+
48					+	+	+	+	+	+	+	+		+
49					+	+	+	+		+	+	+		+
50					+	+	+	+	+	+	+	+		+
51								+	+	+	+	+		+
52					+	+	+							
53								+		+		+		
54	+	+	+	+				+	+	+	+	+	+	
55		+	+	+					-	+	+	+	-	
56			+							+		+		
57	+	+	+	+	+	+	+	+	+	+	+	+	+	+
58	+	+	+	+	+	+	+	+	+	+	+	+	+	+
59	-	-	-	-				-	+	-	-	-	-	
60	d	d	r	d				bl	d	br. r	be. r	r.c	r	
61		s.d												
62			sm	sm						sm		sm	sm	
63	M	M	M	M	?	?	?		M	F	M	M	M	?
	A	A	A	A	A	A	A	A	A	A	A	A	A	Y
	170 175	170 180	170 180	175	25	27 16		180 190	165 170	180	175	175	18 0	15 10

Individual Synthesis

			M	F	Y				M	F	Y
1	20/20	100%	+	+	+	36	7/7	100%	+	?	?
2	10/10	100%	+	+	+	37	15/15	100%	+	+	+
3	16/16	100%	+	+	+	38	16/16	100%	+	+	+
4	4/6	16%	±	+	+	39	15/15	100%	+	+	+
5	2/2	100%	+	?+	+	40	9/9	100%	+	?	+
6	20/20	100%	+	+	+	41	2/2	100%	+	?	?
7	6/6	100%	+	+	+	42	6/6	100%	+	?	?
8	17/18	94%	±	+	+	43	12/14	86%	±	+	+
9	17/17	100%	+	+	+	44	16/17	94%	+	+	+
10	10/10	100%	+	?+	?+	45	7/7	100%	+	?	+
11	9/9	100%	+	+	+	46	18/18	100%	+	+	+
12	10/10	100%	+	+	+	47	24/25	96%	+	+	+
13	10/10	100%	+	+	+	48	14/14	100%	+	+	+
14	7/7	100%	+	+	+	49	10/10	100%	+	?	+
15	10/10	100%	+	+	+	50	14/14	100%	+	+	+
16	3/7	43%	±	?±	?±	51	11/11	100%	+	+	+
17	3/4	75%	±	?±	?±	52	3/3	100%	+	?	?
18	10/11	91%	+	+	-	53	6/6	100%	+	?	?
19	12/12	100%	+	+	+	54	16/16	100%	+	+	+
20	12/12	100%	+	+	+	55	12/15	80%	+	-	-
21	3/3	100%	+	?+	+	56	7/7	100%	+	?	+
22	10/10	100%	+	+	+	57	27/27	100%	+	+	+
23	7/7	100%	+	+	+	58	27/27	100%	+	+	+
24	7/7	100%	+	?+	+	59			-	+	-
25	10/10	100%	+	+	+						
26	9/9	100%	+	?+	+	61		st.d ?st.d			
27	6/6	100%	+	?+	+						
28	11/17	65%	±	+	-	Height		175 169			
29	17/18	95%	+	+	+						
30	16/16	100%	+	+	+						
31	13/15	87%	+	±	?						
32	18/18	100%	+	+	?						
33	18/18	100%	+	+	+						
34	15/16	94%	+	+	+						
35	17/17	100%	+	+	+						

Chapter 2

The Creatures of the Caucasus

In the Caucasus Mountains, which separate Europe from the Middle East, live manlike creatures of which the outside world knows nothing.

Throughout the "taiga", or boreal conifer forests which stretch from Scandinavia to the Bering Sea and beyond, come reports of animals not unlike the famous North American bigfoot. However, the creatures of the Caucasus appear to be a little smaller, a little more manlike, and a little more social.

As the following translation reveals, Russians first became aware of them after hearing news of the Himalayan "abominable snowmen", and researchers over there still refer to their subjects as "snowmen". In this field, the leading lights were Boris Porshnev, surgeon, soldier, and mountaineer, and Marie-Jeanne Koffman[11]. At the time of writing (2020), she is still alive, having celebrated her 100th birthday the previous year in a Paris nursing home. (Update: she passed away on 11 July 2021, just 8 days short of here 102nd birthday.)

Porshnev died in 1972, but Koffmann continued to make personal expeditions to the Caucasus, and in 1991 she wrote a 19-page article in the French journal, *Archéologia*, a translation of which follows. The Caucasus is a refuge, not only for wildlife from many different zones, but also of ethnic groups and languages, and each language has a different word for the animals. Koffmann settled on the Kabardian term, *almasty*. This is perhaps unfortunate, since it invites confusion with the *almas* of Mongolia - which may well be a similar animal, but it is certainly a completely unrelated word. (Note that, in Mongolian, *almas* is singular; it is not the plural of *alma*.) She also refers to them as "hominoids", which simple means "manlike".

. . . .

---

[11] The interview she gave in 1988 provides some background on her life - though not the six years she spent in prison, a victim of Stalin's last purge. See http://www.bigfootencounters.com/interviews/koffmann.htm

The Almasty, Yeti of the Caucasus
by
Marie-Jeanne Koffmann

Archéologia **no. 269, June 1991, pp 24-43**

Prehistorians build their science starting from discoveries of which the most notorious concern a practically complete skeleton or a body fragment. For once, in the following years, are they going to observe a hominid, a fossil survivor from prehistory? The almasty, or wild man of the Caucasus, would be the object of this prodigious observation. Different from the yeti of the Himalayas, which is only a *Gigantopithecus*, the almasty of the Caucasus already possesses certain characteristics of Neanderthal man. Formerly rather familiar to the inhabitants of the region, who retain numerous memories of their encounters with the wild men, it is unfortunately on the road to disappearance. The Russian archaeologists who are actively trying to observe it have not yet succeeded in approaching it. This exceptional perspective will hold the breath of the specialists in evolution in the course of the following years and perhaps one day will achieve their expectation.

The enquiry undertaken over several years among the numerous populations of the Caucasus has permitted one to draw up a dossier of the more than 500 declarations by witnesses, affirming they have personally observed, often over long periods of time, bipedal, hairy, hominoid creatures, lacking any language, and designated in the local languages as "forest men" or "wild men".

The analysis of the descriptions of the "wild men" reveal extremely precise anatomic, ecological and ethnological criteria. This evidence, along with certain observations collected in the field, permits one to suppose that these hominoid creatures really exist.

The publication in 1956 in the Soviet press of the Anglo-American researches in the Himalayas concerning hairy, bipedal creatures called "Yetis", immediately provoked an abundant mail, addressed by the mountainous provinces of the USSR, to the scientific authorities, and to the editors of the major newspapers. Schoolmasters, doctors, shepherds, servicemen, were amazed at the interest shown by foreign expeditions, as well as the USSR itself, in manlike creatures similar to those they knew well, which left Soviet science indifferent.

Such writings did not move the scientists at all. As luck had it, however, Professor B. Porshnev gave it attention. World famous historian, philosopher, and humanist (doctor *honoris causa*, among others, of the Montpellier University) Porshnev was seized by the simplicity of the accounts, the realism of the descriptions, and with all the concordances, despite the diversity of sources.

The energy and authority of Professor Porshnev was able to overcome the resistance, indeed indignation, of the academic body. Brought to the consideration of the Presidium of the USSR Academy of Sciences, the debate lead to the creation, close to the Presidium in January 1958, of a Commission of study on the problem of "the snowman", and the organisation of a research expedition to the Pamir, entrusted to the Botanical Institute of the Academy, which possessed its own scientific base there, and whose collaborators claimed to be informed of the existence of strange manlike beings. The USSR was thus the only country to attempt a serious exploration of this unsolved problem.

The Commission displayed an intense activity: bibliographic researches which must have brought to the light of day numerous descriptions of these creatures by naturalists and explorers of every era and place; having alerted the Chinese authorities about them, they received communications of a lot of information about their western territories, such that a joint Sino-Soviet expedition was projected for 1959; collaboration with the Academy of Sciences of Mongolia, of which two eminent members had been applied to the problem in the 1920s, as well as with the Western zoologists who had revealed the existence of the yetis or directed the Himalayan expeditions (Doctors B. Heuvelmans and G. Russell in France, I. Sanderson in the USA); an annual edition of booklets presenting, without commentaries, nor retouched, the information such as arrived from different parts of the world or from the depths of time.

The Pamir expedition met a check, and closed down. Conceived rather precociously in the burst of initial enthusiasm, the 1958 expedition of the Academy of Sciences, of which I was the doctor, was premature. This check was vigorously exploited by the powerful "opposition", and the Commission slowly wound up by itself by 1960. Henceforth, the research was in the hands of a few particular people bereft of all material, technical, and financial means, a situation singularly difficult in the USSR, where all activity is structured by the State.

The Academy of Sciences agreed, however, to edit, in 1963, the voluminous monograph, "Current status of the problem of relic hominoids", where Porshnev exposed and analysed the exceptional documentation gathered to that date on these bipeds of hominoid demeanour, spread out over certain regions of the globe, and advanced the hypothesis of their paleoanthropological nature.

It is then that the Caucasus arose.

After 1958, the Presidium of the Academy had received the official visit of a lieutenant-colonel doctor, Dr. V. Karapetian, who felt it was his duty to advise them of an incongruent personal observation, which the recent publication of at last permitted interpretation: in the winter of 1941, in Daghestan, he had been called up to examine a being of human appearance, male, covered by a thick fleece, and with a bestial expression, which had been intercepted by a military patrol.[12] Shortly afterwards, a similar declaration was deposed by the Chief Inspector of Hunting of the Republic of Daghestan, K. Leontiev. In August 1958, he had observed for a few seconds, on a high mountain, an identical creature. He described in minute detail its footprints, resting on a slab of snow.

Almost simultaneously, we discovered a piece of analogous information. Dated 1899, it came from an illustrious zoologist, Professor Satunin, whose work on the Caucasian fauna remains exhaustive: he caught a glimpse of a "hairy wild woman" in the course of an expedition to the eastern Caucasus. One should note that these three persons were all foreign to the Caucasus, and especially qualified to judge a zoological phenomenon.

Nevertheless, these first Caucasian communications aroused a deep confusion. The idea of the survival to the 20th century of an unknown hominoid population appeared absurd and unacceptable. The research on the "snowman" was taking a ridiculous turn ... As an alpinist, and a former combatant of the Battle of the Caucasus in 1942, I decided in August 1959 to leave for the southern slopes of the Great Caucasus, bordering on Daghestan, with the intention of casting light on the problem.

Then, a month later, I returned to Moscow, holding verbal declarations of 40 witnesses who had personally observed the "men of the forest". Research on relic hominoids in the Caucasus had led me, on foot, by horse, and in automobiles, across practically all of the republics:

---

[12] Eventually, the C.O., with typical Soviet paranoia, had it shot as a spy.

Azerbaijan, Georgia, Daghestan, Chechnya-Ingushia, Ossetia, Kabardino-Balkharia, Karachai, Circassia, the territories of Stavropol, and in Kuban. This research has been pursued over many years.

While I did not believe at the start in the existence of these hominoids unknown to scholars, I was progressively led to change my opinion thanks to the result of a vast enquiry among diverse strata of Caucasian populations, and some material vestiges: beds, alimentary remains, excrement, and footprints.

THE CAUCASUS

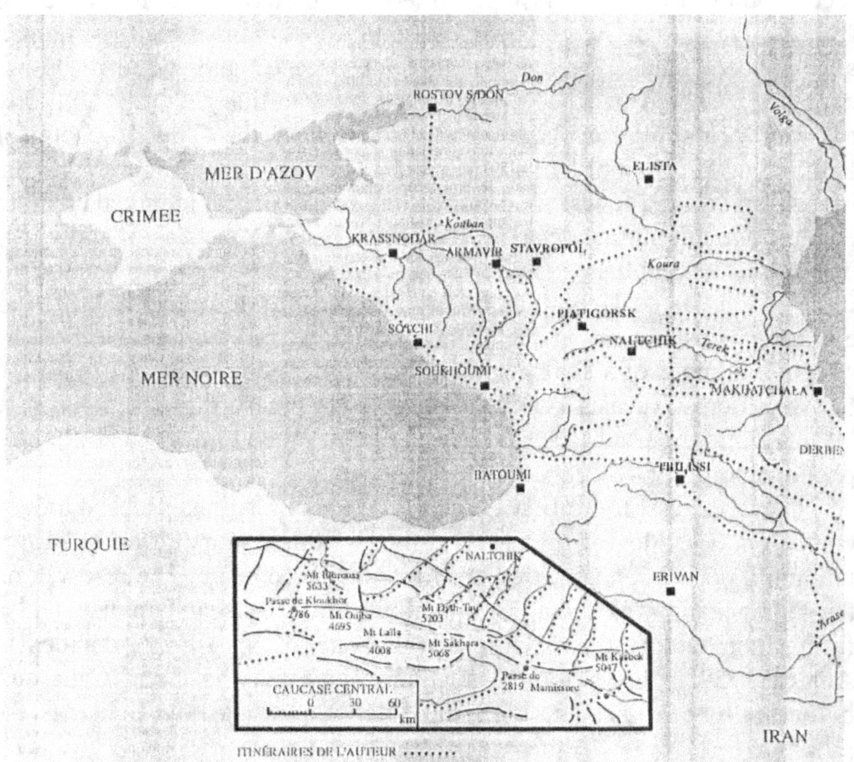

Map of the Caucasus, with the author's itinerary as a dotted line (labelled in French)

Stretching from the steppes of southern Russia to the great plateaux of Anatolia, Armenia and Iran, the Caucasus occupies the whole of the isthmus separating the Black Sea and the Caspian, covering a surface of

440,000 km^2, or 4/5 that of France. A portion of the great geosyncline which must have given birth to the string of mountains stretching from Spain to the Himalayas, the Caucasus shares its rolling destiny. By turns, a tropical isle bathed by the warm Tethys Sea and an archipelago, it is to these episodes that it owes the endemism of a part of its current flora and fauna. The raising of the Lower Caucasus in the Miocene transformed the archipelago into a peninsula, into which flowed the fauna of the Near East, but also that of Central Asia, the Mediterranean Basin, and Eastern Europe.

The Quarterary, drying out the rest of the Thetys Sea, opened the route to the Caucasus to the northern flora and fauna. The essential geomorphological element of the region is the Great Caucasus, which crosses the isthmus diagonally, an immense, uninterrupted barrier 1,200 km long, 120 to 150 km wide, and 3,000 to 5,000 metres high [18,510 ft]. Fifteen summits reach or pass 5,000 metres; the Elbrus, an ancient volcano peaks at 5,642 metres. The barrier consists of several chains, sometimes parallel, sometimes twisted among themselves, circumscribing deep depressions, extremely difficult to access, veritable microcosms. The part called the North Caucasus, or Ciscaucasia, is a gradual slope towards the watershed of waters flowing northwards from the Great Caucasus, with a temperate, humid climate; Transcaucasia, falling abruptly and also part of the isthmus, to the south of the large chains, has a subtropical climate. The extraordinary diversity of the Caucasian sites – powerful mountainous edifices, sandy deserts crossed by camels, inaccessible canyons, dense northern forests or veritable jungles, vertiginous cuestas, continental plateaux, the littoral

Riviera of the Black Sea, the marshes of the ancient Colchis – is equaled only by that of the fauna and plants. To cite only the most common animals: bear, fox, wolf, lynx, wild cat, wild boar, ibex, chamois, deer, bison, together with tiger (alas, now practically extinct), leopard, hyena, jackal, saiga, gazelle, later wild goat, porcupine *etc*. Among the paleontological ancestry, one should note a Tertiary anthropoid ape, *Udabnopithecus* (end of the Miocene, beginning of the Pliocene).

The mosaic of the innumerable Caucasian peoples – Strabo had already counted three hundred – makes the Caucasus one of the most complex regions of the world, ethnologically speaking. Inhabited since the Paleolithic, the theatres of the earliest civilisations (Urartu, 10th century B.C.), the Caucasus has been especially the site of of thousands of years of confrontations between Paleo-Caucasians, Assyrians, Medes, Persians, Romans, Parthians, Ottomans, and Byzantines. Then at the foot of its northern slopes broke waves of Cimmerians, Scythians, Alans, Huns, Khazars, Mongols, and who knows how many other peoples. Each wave of assailants exterminated in blood and fire the preceding populations, of which some refugees would sometimes find safety in the depths of the high mountains where, some decades later, they would by joined by survivors of a new massacre, perpetuated by a third invader. Aborigines, Semites, Iranians, Indo-Europeans, Mongols, pagans, Sabeans, fire worshipers, Lamaists, adepts of Judaism, Christians and Muslims, thus found themselves gathered together in this Babel of languages (Daghestan alone counts more than forty), always guarding their individuality.

In spite of this multiplicity of origins, the very characteristic type of Caucasian permits immediate recognition. Against a background of poorly controlled emotionality and spontaneity, they bear witness to an extreme simplicity of human relations and of acceptance of the world, the stamp of a sense of justice and dignity, boundless hospitality, the veneration of aged persons and, above all, a guest, this being associated with much carelessness, versatility, and ingenuity. In fact, the Caucasian peoples are fully marked with the very seal of traditions of archaic common beliefs, jealously conserved or imposed by the identical conditions of existences of small feudal societies living essentially by breeding and brigandage. Soviet power conferred on all these ethnic groups an administrative structure, a cultural apparatus, an alphabet (only Armenia and Georgia possessed their own literature), abolishing and severely repressing the rape of women, blood feud, warlike incursions for livestock raiding, and ethnic confrontations. Difficult customs to renounce, especially when the police, sons of the same people, understand the situation so well ... Still today, the Caucasian retains of many things the innocent viewpoint of simple peoples.

THE TESTIMONIES

Out of 500 eyewitness testimonies, Dr Koffmann chose to publish twelve. In reading them, you should keep in mind a number of reservations.

Firstly, it is unlikely that all of the witnesses spoke Russian. It is likely that many of the testimonies were provided by means of an interpreter. Secondly, this was the Soviet Union. Having a Russian interviewer taking down notes on a clip-board was probably not the best way to get a Caucasian to "open up". It is likely, therefore, that these testimonies were written up by memory after the interview was terminated. (On the other hand, considering that she had 500 reports to choose from, these might just be the exceptions to the rule. It is evident that some of the witnesses were prominent men.) Thirdly, as European folklorists have discovered, if you visit places where people still believe in fairies, you will find people who claim to have seen them. It is possible, therefore, that some of these stories are fictitious. On the other hand, one must also consider the uniformity of the testimonies across ethnic boundaries, as well as collateral evidence, such as footprints.

Finally, quite apart from the normal increase in human population, this area has been, and continues to be, the site of bitter internecine strife. In view of this, I can only feel disturbed by noting that very few of these reports date from the 1950s or later. There are also frequent references to their being more common in the past. Is man's closest relative going extinct before it is even recognized by science? (This is a fear expressed by more recent researchers, although close-up sightings are still being reported.)

. . . .

Dr. Koffmann has at her disposal the declarations of more than 500 witnesses affirming that they have personally observed these creatures. Of very diverse nationalities, age, levels of education, and social class, the informants are, by and large, simple men: shepherds, peasants, drivers. Their knowledge of nature and their faculty of observation are undeniable. Second hand information is numerous, and is not included in this list. It goes without saying that the name of the creatures described varies with the language of the country. It is always translated as "man of the woods" (*méchae-adame* in Azerbaijani, *chiss katsi* in Georgian, *agach-kishi* in Karachai, etc), "wild man", or "hairy man". She uses the Kabardian *almasty*, with which she is familiar, since it is especially Kabardino-Bakharia, at the foot of the Elbrus, which serves as the basis of her researches.

The data are of unequal volume and value with respect to the circumstances of the observation, duration, distance, clarity, the interest displayed by the witness, his state of fear or curiosity, and the position and behaviour of the almasty. One witness will be struck by a secondary detail and will obstinately return to it, scornful of the essential details; his neighbour will insist on a completely different aspect; a third will have been able to examine the creatures at leisure and on several occasions, to approach them, or give them food. Here are some examples of reports, chosen among hundreds in the possession of the author. Taken in isolation, each of these communications have no value, but collected in the hundreds, they constitute a dossier of which the existence can be established as factual.

THREE ALMASTIES UNDER A ROCK

Report of Kumychev Talib, 67, Kabardian, one of the most respected elders of the village of Kammeromost, in the Republic of Kabardino-Balkaria (the text of the report is abridged).

… It was approximately in 1930, or 1931, or 1932, in June or the end of May, when our cattle departed for the alpine pastures of Elbrus. I was the team leader. We were leaving to inspect the herds with the zootechnician.

... Well, the rain had surprised one of my shepherds, Zagureev Shagir, very high on the slope. He went to seek refuge under a rocky overhang where, on approaching, he saw three seated almasties. Shagir was a bit scared, but the rain was getting heavier, so he decided to stay, just the same, under the shelter, merely keeping to the side. Then the rain having cleared, Shagir went down to the farm. He said nothing to anyone.

Very early in the morning, I was awakened by shouts, a great voice, and I saw two shepherds collecting their flocks on the run and driving the cattle down into the valley.

"Where are they going?" I asked.

"There are almasties under the rock, up there."

... At that moment, Shagir declared: "That's right. There are three almasties sitting up there; I saw them yesterday evening."

I was definitely furious... I said to Shagir: "You're an imbecile. You were afraid of a bush."

"No," said Shagir, "I saw them."

"Then, why didn't you say so?"

"Because the elders say: when you see the almasty for the first time, if you tell anybody, you will get a headache. And for me, that was the first time I saw any."

I still did not believe. Someone said to me, "Well, go and see for yourself."

There were about ten to fifteen of us making a semicircle around that rock. We stayed there until dinner. Some left, others arrived. Three almasties were sitting under the overhang, two of medium height, the other bigger. The biggest was in the middle. They were sitting on the stones facing us, bent over, their heads low. From time to time, they raised their head slightly and looked at us down below. Their heads were very ugly, not attractive.

The face resembles that of a human to some extent, but the nose is shorter and flattened. The eyes are slanted and reddish. The cheeks project a lot, like those of a Mongol or Korean – even more so. The lips are thin. The lower jaw appears cut off and sloping.

The hair of the head is long, like that of a woman, and tangled. The whole body is covered with hair recalling that of a buffalo. As to location, it is longer on the torso and chest, shorter on the arms and legs.

The big one had the chest of a man. The others had women's breasts, but extremely long and covered with hair.

The body hair was very dirty. The stench was such, that one couldn't stand it. The odour recalled that of wild flax, when it is growing densely.

At one point, the one on the right mumbled something.

I did not see their hands very well; they were clenched between their legs. The legs are a little short and bowed. The foot is like that of a man's, but more splayed.

All wore, rolled around their loins, an old piece of shepherd's cape. A young shepherd proposed to throw an *ancane* (a sort of lasso) onto one of them and lead it to the village. But all the others cried out that this was forbidden, that he must not do them harm, that he must not disturb them.

I was looking at them from a distance of three or four metres [10 to 13 ft]. I even approached to within a metre. If I had touched them. Don't think of it! If you were to touch one, as Allah is my witness, you would not eat with your hands afterwards, they were so dirty, stinking, and repulsive.

I stayed close to two hours. When I left, some of the other shepherds arrived.

[...] I have heard my father tell that they suck from the cows."

LOVERS OF HEMP SEED AND WATER MELONS

Report of Koshokoev Erzhib, 70, Kabardian, inhabitant of Circassian Stary

"Before the war, there were many almasties at our home; one could say, masses. Today, it appears one meets very few. Personally, I have seen them three times.

The first time was in October 1944. Our detachment (of servicemen) was riding through a field of hemp, on the steppe ... Suddenly, the horse of the first horseman halted so abruptly that I almost jostled him; I was riding second in line. He said to me: "Look! An almasty!" In front of us, a few yards away, an almasty was thrusting into its mouth the ends of hemp stems containing the seeds. Behind us, the detachment was bunching up, making noise. She noticed us and ran very fast – she ran extraordinarily quickly – towards a shepherd's hut, which was not far away. While she was running, several men in our detachment pulled down their rifles from their shoulders and were preparing to fire, but our leader, a Russian officer from Nalchik, shouted: "Don't shoot, don't shoot! Let's take it alive and bring it to Nalchik!"

We dismounted and surrounded the shepherd's hut. We were very numerous and we were able to close the circle around the hut. I was just opposite the door and could see very well. While we were approaching, the almasty left two or three times, in one bound, out of the hut. She appeared very agitated: she left, fussed about, threw herself from one side to another; but on noticing me, she jumped back inside, left again immediately from another side, but there again saw the people. In doing this, she grimaced, her lips moving very fast, very fast, and she mumbled something.

In the meantime, our cordon was closing in. We had closed ranks and were advancing elbow to elbow. At that moment, the almasty appeared again, shook itself in all directions and, suddenly, let out a terrible cry and rushed straight onto the men. She ran faster than a horse. To tell the truth, the men were surprised and frightened. She easily broke through our cordon, jumped into the ravine, and disappeared into the undergrowth surrounding the river.

She measured about 1.80 m [5 ft 11], very robust. It was difficult to see her face because of the hair. The breasts hung down the belly. She was covered with long reddish hair, like that of a buffalo. You could easily see through the scraps of old, man-made Kabardian kaftan, which she was wearing, all tattered.

It is necessary to watch out for almasties at night, close to the hemp fields, when it is ripening. The hemp, they love it. They eat a lot of it. They go around the whole field, consuming the heads of grain. In doing so, they constantly mumble, "Boom, boom, boom", they chew noisily, they blow through their noses, they rustle the stems. When the almasty is eating hemp, you hear it from afar, at night. How may times, in season, I have heard them mumble like that. These last years, I have never heard them any more.

Almasties also like water melons. Previously, they used to come into the plantations and wreak a lot of havoc. I have a friend, an old man; he used to be a guard on a melon patch in the collective farm; he lived in a hut. One day, I was going to see him and I noted that a lot of water melons had been spoiled, nibbled in a peculiar manner, eaten from the middle. [...] I took one of them and saw the marks of big teeth. I understood that it had been an almasty.

I reached my friend, laughed, and said to him: "A fine guard you are! Look, your plantation, what has become of it!" He replied: "Shut up! This almasty is wearing me down. Every night, he comes to eat the water melons. I go out to meet him with my club, but I don't dare approach too close. I yell out at him: 'You have no shame! Go away!' He says to me: 'Boom, boom, boom." I yell out again: 'You have no conscience! Me, I am the guard! I am responsible for the melons.' He answers me: 'Boom, boom, boom.' And there you are, we chat like that all night."

Do you know of cases where someone has killed an almasty or recovered a corpse?

Thirty or forty years ago, two shepherds came and told how they had found a quite fresh almasty corpse in the forest, devoured by wolves or dogs. In fact, there was nothing left of the corpse but the head. The shepherds were desolate. They kept repeating, "It is very sad! It is very sad!"

Why do certain almasties wear human clothes?

First of all, one has pity on the almasties. Previously, it used to happen that the almasties would come into the houses for someone to feed them. At the same time, a person would dress them so that they would not get cold.

Then the almasties would help themselves. That used to happen very often formerly: someone would go to the forest or into the fields, to gather wood or mow some hay; he would hang up on a branch his provisions and the clothes which were too hot to wear. He would return a few hours later: his provisions would have been eaten, and his clothes would have disappeared; the almasties had stolen the lot.

The almasties used to observe man very attentively. For example, a man walks into the forest. He feels hot. He sees a river. He undresses, spreads out his effects on the bank, and bathes. Then, he dresses and goes away. At the same time, just as he has left, at the very minute, out of the forest comes the almasty, of course, if there were one in the neighbourhood. Obligatorily, it approaches the spot where the clothes had been deposited, it feels the ground, it sniffs it. The almasty is very curious.

EATEN BY DOGS

The tale of Kumykov Feitsa, 67, Kabardian from Kurkuzhin

"Almasties, I have seen a lot of them. How many times? If you want me to tell you, I would see them all the time for five years, in the summer, when I was in the mountain meadows. It was in the 1930s, in the direction of the Elbus, in a rocky place, where there were caves. There used to be many almasties in this region; they used to go into the caves and exit them like bees in a hive, very tall, taller than us; but I only ever saw them one at a time.

They were of different ages; some smaller, some larger. I think there were more women than men. With the men, the testicles were placed well in the rear, as with a boar. I never saw a newborn but I have often heard them crying. The oldtimers say that the women find the means to attach them to the chest.

The almasties are like us; they have arms and legs, but they are hairy. Their hair is like a bear's, dark. I always saw them naked; I never saw them wear clothes. They cannot speak, they only mumble or bellow. They are not afraid of people, only dogs. They run very fast.

They always used to come very early in the morning or once the sun had set – because they are afraid of dogs – to lick the gems of salt, close to our shelter. I often saw them do it, almost every day. They would come when the sheep were not there, and the dogs had left with them.

Twice, in that period, I saw them quite close. One day, I was returning to the village. I had a small bag of food: cheese, bread, and a piece of mutton. Towards evening it began to rain heavily. I entered a cave, lit a wood fire, and stretched out my woollen cape. At night, the rain intensified. Suddenly, something very big entered the cave, covered in reddish hair, on two legs. At that moment, I believed it was a bear, and then, no, I saw it was an almasty. I was very scared. I was not armed; I had only my dagger. I pretended to see nothing, but I was more dead than alive. I was holding my dagger in my right hand, concealed next to me so that it would not see it, and would not become angry. Then, I calmed down a bit. I recalled that the old people always said that, if you do them no harm, they never attack a human being. However, the almasty sat down next to the fire, to the side, and began to squeeze the water out of its hair, for it was soaked. It took it like this. [Kumykov takes a wick of hair between his two fists, and squeezed it towards his arm, the hairs being dried by pressure.] Then, it settled down close to the fire, offering first one side and then the other. Finally, it sank down almost at my feet. I cautiously moved off a little to the side, but it stretched out once more on my feet, and like that, little by little, effectively pushed me away from the fire. I was completely reassured, because I could see that it was not evil. Besides, it was a female; she had very long breasts, which hung along her belly. I said a few words to it, I tried to speak to it in Kabardian, in Balkar, and in Russian. But it only mumbled some incomprehensible sounds.

I was beginning to feel sleepy; it was already very late. But I did not dare. I ended up dozing off, lying on my left side. At night, I could hear it chomping and chewing. I thought about my provisions. I heard it sucking the bones, but I said nothing.

In the morning, I woke up very early, but it was already gone. My bag was untied and empty. She had eaten everything; she left me nothing. The mutton bones were carefully lined up next to the bag.

The other time, it happened like this. I had left with two donkeys to try my luck at booty in a hut of some absent Balkar neighbours, not far from our shepherd's quarters, in the bushes. Our four dogs, big Caucasian shepherds, were following me. It was evening.

Then, as we go closer, the dogs suddenly rushed forward and began to run around the hut barking. As if there was someone inside. I approached the door, and cautiously opened it. In the middle of the hut stood an almasty. I remained at the door, and the almasty looked at me, its lips quivering rapidly. It should have stayed, for I would never have allowed the dogs to do it harm. But it was probably scared. Abruptly, it leaped towards the door and ran away, bumping into my left shoulder. I almost fell over. My shoulder ached for a month. It ran on two legs, very fast, screaming in a very sharp, very loud voice, like a woman. I tried to hold back the dogs, I yelled, I called. In vain. The dogs returned two or three hours later, tired out, with blood-stained jaws and paws, but nevertheless without a scratch on them. Thus, they had torn it to pieces. Dogs do not tolerate almasties.

What does it eat, the almasty? It eats the afterbirths of cattle, torn horses, carrion. It goes there where a man relieves himself. It eats hellebore. I have heard the old folks say that and I have seen myself that they consume a lot.

THE OCCUPANT OF THE VEGETABLE GARDEN

The tale of Pshukov Mohamed, 40, Kabardian, mason, inhabitant of Kyzburun

It was in 1939 or 1940, in summer ... Where she came from, I do not know, but one day, a (female) almasty turned up in our vegetable garden and installed herself in the maize patch. She made herself a bed there of some old rags and grass. She spent a week at our place, without ever leaving the garden. She used to eat the green maize. She was completely covered with hair. Her (head) hair was very long. The breasts were extended, they hung down like a woman's, but very low. The nails were long. The eyes were bridled, and red. The teeth were larger than a man's, the lips were those of an ape's.

During the day, she always used to remain lying down. In general, she would lie on her side, but she would turn around all the time, she did not keep the same position for long.

Many people used to come to our place to see her. If several people approached at once, she would become disturbed, sit up, cry out, and tear her (head) hair. She would cry out very loud, like a woman.

When she calmed down, if there was anyone near her, she would approach very gently, and start to lick him like a dog. When you left, the sleeve of your shirt would be quite wet.

NOISY NEIGHBOURS

The report of Khakonov Danial, 65, pensioner, Kabardian of Karmakovo

When I used to work as a shepherd in the Akbecheyiko Valley, at the very shepherd's hut where you were this morning, I used to see almasties all the time. It was in the 1940s. One evening, at the end of October, we were cooking some meat. At that moment, the sheep scattered. We ran to gather them back. When we returned an hour later, another pot. It was a pot of about fifteen litres [>3 gallons]. What do you think? You think nothing: you know it was the almasties. Not far from us stood an old hut. Almasties lived there. How many? I don't know. A whole family, probably: six or seven. We used to hear them making noise every day, towards evening: they move around, fight, play. They are very noisy people, who squall, yell, weep. They don't have any human language, they speak like a drum: "Boom-boom-boom!" None of us would go into that house. One day, I proposed a sheep to anyone who would shift himself there, but no-one wanted to go. They, on the other hand, used to come into our shepherd's hut and take the remains of our food.

One day, they pulled into their house a length of guttering which was trailing in the ground. All night, they played with this guttering. They were living it up and did not let us sleep during the night. We were five men, with rifles, but we were scared to go and see what they were doing. The pot, we recovered it the following morning, empty of course, but far away, between the stream and their house.

I worked three years in that corner. They were there all the time, especially in summer. Our dogs became used to them, they growled, but didn't touch them. However, if the dogs surrounded one the almasty would cry out loudly.

I have often seen their footprints: five toes, no arch, round heel, broad sole. They look a bit like the prints of a bear.

I have not been back there since 1947.

THE NOCTURNAL MEAL

The Report of Didaov Dina, 40, Kabardian, electrician at Baxan
In the summer of 1950, I was sent to make an inventory of the farms
in the alpine pastures of the Elbrus. Towards midnight, I went to bed.
The shelter consisted of three stone walls. There was no fourth wall; it
was open. Everyone went to bed on the ground, on the hay, under our
woollen capes, head to the end wall, feet towards the outside. I was lying
at the edge. Between the side wall and me, there remained a space where
we had laid out the pot of broth and a saucepan of grilled meat.

Everyone fell asleep quickly. Me, I was young, a little excited by
the conversation, the meal, the unfamiliar ambiance – that was the first
time I had gone to bed in the mountains – and I didn't fall asleep. My
neighbour, an old man, did not sleep for long. At times, he would doze
off, then wake up, smoke, and go back to sleep.

Suddenly, some sort of woman came quickly and silently into the
shelter. Hideous, with hair hanging to her waist. She stared at the wall
where a bridle was hanging, a Caucasian bridle adorned with metallic
pendants. She directly took down the bridle, turned it around, turned it
around again, examined it from all sides, hung it back up on the wall, and
silently went away. I was paralysed with fear. Just the same, the old man
wasn't sleeping. I asked him: "What was that?" He calmly replied: "It's
nothing to be concerned about. If you stay here, you'll see a lot more like
that." And he went back to sleep.

Suddenly, she reappeared, halted motionless, examined the sleeping
men attentively, quickly approached the saucepans, and placed herself
one or two yards from me.

The pot was closed with its lid and the frying pan, like at home,
with another pan. She crouched down, quickly and silently lifted the lid
and the frying pan, and began to eat. She ate any old how, sometimes the
meat from the frying pan sometimes the broth. She imbibed the broth
with big wooden dipper which she had taken from the lid. She did not
hold it like a human being, but with all the fingers on one side. Her
fingers were very long, except for the thumb, which was shorter than in a
human being. Her countenance was hideous, not beautiful. Completely
hairy, with dark brown hair covering the whole of her body. Long breasts
hanging to her belly. The head hair loose, long, tangled. The nose was
small, not upturned, as this man said, but flattened. The mouth was very
broadly split, a lot more than ours, the lips were thin, like an ape's. The

skin was black. The cheeks jutted out, as with the Chinese or Koreans. But there are Chinese and Chinese. Some have prominent cheeks, others less so. Hers were very strong, like a real, authentic Chinese. Her eyes were strongly bridled, and their colour was thus: if, in place of eyes, you put little pocket-light bulbs and placed a red glass in front, this would be her eyes exactly.

She wore some sort of dress, all torn and disgusting. She ate sitting down on her heels, very fast, seizing with very fast movements, sometimes meat, sometimes soup. She chewed very quickly; you couldn't tell whether she was chewing or swallowing whole. But she ate very attentively, without ceasing for a second in looking to the right and left.

What struck me, it was the speed, precision, and silence of her movements. Word of honour, if I were to start to eat, for example, I would certainly make a noise, I would have bumped into something. Her, she does everything in silence. Just like a silent movie. For example, when she took the bridle. The bridle carried national decorations in metal; they naturally clatter. Well, she took it down and hung it up again without the least noise.

When she had finished eating, she quickly and quietly closed the pot with its lid, and the pan with the pan, she replaced the wooden dipper on the lid exactly on the spot where she had found it, and went away.

If I had been alone, I would have probably died of fright. But, although I was scared, I felt reassured, because there was a lot of world. I told myself, if something happens, I will start to cry out, and they will all get up. I did not fall asleep for a long time. In the morning, everyone began to eat the meat and the broth, and offered some to me. I refused; I had seen who had eaten it at night. I said that I did not normally eat in the morning.

THE DEAD ALMASTY

The account of Zhigunov Khazrail Khamid, 46, Kabardian, brickyard batcher from Baxan.

"At the end of September 1939 or 1940, I was following the road from Nizhny Kukuzhin to Malka. I decided to cut across an immense field of maize. Scarcely had I left the road, forty yards from it, when I fell upon the remains of an almasty devoured by wolves or dogs. Over a clearing of about a dozen yards in diameter, completely trampled down, the maize was knocked over and ravaged. In the middle of this zone lay the head of the almasty with what remained of the neck. The left half of the neck had been devoured. Up to that day, I did not believe in the existence of almasties. I used to laugh and asserted that they were fables, inventions. That was why I proceeded to the examination of this head with particular interest. Armed with a stick, I turned it over on all sides and, seated on my heels, I examined it attentively. The head was completely enveloped in a crop of very long hair which, in the living state, would have probably reached the waist; it was very much entangled and cemented with thistles. This crop of hair was so thick that, when I turned over the head, it remained in the air, like a cushion. That was why I could not discern the shape of the skull. But the dimensions were those of a human skull. The brow was recessive. This spot jutted out a lot (he pointed to the superciliary arch). The nose was small, trumpeted. It had no root, it was like pushed into the face. It was the nose of an ape. The cheek bones jutted out like a Chinese's. The lips were not those of a man's; they were thin and straight like an ape's. I did not see the teeth; the lips were tightly clenched. The chin was not like a man's, but rounded and heavy. The ears were human; one was torn, the other intact. The eyes were strongly bridled, the slit was directed down and outwards. I do not know the colour of the eyes; the lids were closed, and I did not open them. The skin was black, covered with dark brown hairs. The hairs were absent around the eyes and on the area above the cheeks. The cheeks themselves and the eyes were covered with short hairs; they were longer on the neck and chin.

There issued from the head a powerful and repulsive odour. It was not the odour of decomposition; the remains were fresh, and felt nothing, there were neither flies nor worms. It was the odour of the almasty itself, so sickening that I almost vomited. Also, I was examining the head and pinching my nostrils with my left hand, while handling my stick with the right. The odour recalled that of a dirty body, of mould.

Nearby lay scattered the other parts of the body; I noticed whitish bones covered with shreds of flesh, but I did not approach them."

Did the almasty's face recall that of a man or an ape's?

"It is very difficult to answer you. The nose and lips were exactly like an ape's. But, evidently, on the whole, the face recalled that of a man."

We show to Zhigunov the "portrait" of Pithecanthropus reconstructed by Burian. Zhigunov recognized a certain resemblance between its nose and that of the almasty. Pointing out the chin, he repeated several times: "Exactly that!" The mouth itself was similar. The eyes and their slit were totally different. On the whole, except for the lower part of the face, he found only a very general resemblance to the almasty.

A BIRTH AMONG THE ALMASTIES

Account of Akhaminov Khuzer Bekanluk, 55, Kabardian, peasant at Planovskoye

"There was one month, 19 August (1964), I was reaping 3 km [2 miles] from the village in a sunflower field where there remained several clearings which had not been sown. I suddenly heard a funny sort of noise like someone breathing noisily. Like a dog, when a fly enters its nose ... When it sounded a third time, I put down my scythe to go and see. Abruptly, two arms, humanlike, but black, hairy, and long, extended out of the grass in my direction. I immediately hurled myself towards my cart, and climbed inside; it was standing unharnessed a dozen yards away. Standing on the cart, I saw a silhouette, humanlike, which, hunched up, was sinking into the sunflowers. I was only able to see well the back, covered with long red hairs like those of a buffalo, and the long hair of the head. I did not see its face. When the almasty had left (I immediately recognized it, because I had seen some before), I climbed down from my cart and returned to the scythe. At that moment, I heard a squalling at the same place. I advanced cautiously and parted the stems.

On some cupped grass, like a nest, two newborns were lying. One could see that they had just been born. They were exactly like suckling humans, except that they were smaller; they would have been no more than two kilos [4.4 lb]. Apart from that, you would not have been able to distinguish them from our little ones. They had pink skin, like human babies, exactly the same head, the same arms and legs. Not hairy. Like humans or newborn rats, you see: pink skinned and naked. They waved their little arms and legs, just like our newborns, squalling.

I ran away. I quickly harnessed my ass and returned to the village. Two or three days afterwards, I returned, but there was nothing."

But why did you tell nobody?

"What do you mean, 'nobody'? I told my wife, and neighbours."

I mean, why did you not make a report?

But, make a report to whom? Why make one?"

To the authorities, to the police, to the soviet! (The idea of making such a futile report – an almasty in childbirth! ... to the authorities roused frank hilarity from the whole little group present.) But, didn't you know that it was of interest, that scholars where concerned about the almasty?

"Who knew it, that it was important, that! In my life, I have never heard it said that anyone would be interested in it."

AN ALMASTY BATHING

Account of Khadji Murat, 23, Azerbaijani, driver at Belokany.

"In the autumn of 1959, I was following, at night, the edge of the Belokany-chai River. I was carrying a bag of rice which I had "deducted" lower down, at the old mill. That would have been twenty-odd kilos [45 lb]. Obviously, I did not wish to meet anybody. As if deliberately, the moon was shining with all its clarity. Also, I was taking, not the main road, but the back streets of the village, along the river. Suddenly, I heard a noisy splashing. At first I believed it was the wind carrying the noise of the waves of the rapids, but there was no wind and then, the rapids were quite small. The splashing was repeating itself regularly, as if someone was emptying a whole bucket in one go. I told myself: "This must be the neighbour opposite, who is bathing; the devil take him. How am I going to pass?"

I was cautiously approaching the river and threw a glance from behind a rock. I perceived, by the moonlight, someone very tall in the water. She was standing upright and throwing enormous globs of water with both hands. "That's funny," I thought. "The neighbour isn't so tall." At that moment, I noticed long hair on its head. "Bah, that's better; it's not the neighbour, it's his wife! Well," I said to myself, "I'm going to go and see her bathe."

I put down my bag and approached with the step of a wolf. I arrived at the bank, but justly, there were bushes which thwarted me; I could not see well. It was necessary to retrace my steps. She was behind a block of stone. I lay down on my belly, crawled towards the rock, and raised my head gently, exactly at the level of the water, just to the side of her ... And at once almost dropped dead. Standing upright in the water was an abominable woman. It wasn't just the face she had, but the frightening maw. Enormous, long hands. She was filling her palms with water and throwing it over her shoulders. Word of honour, it was half a bucket she was collecting each time. Then, she grabbed her breasts and began to throw they on the water. Now, her breasts were very long, enormous, and they splashed dully on the water. Then, she began again to slosh herself.

My hair was standing on end. I slowly crawled back, then I jumped to my feet, and ran across the road to the neighbour, the same one I believed his wife or he was bathing. For a long time I knocked at his door. Finally, he came out. I said to him: "Get your rifle, and let's run quick; there's a kaptar bathing, come and see." [*Kaptar* is the Azeri name for the almasty.] At first, he hesitated; finally, we left. When we had arrived, there was no-one about.

The neighbour helped me to transport the rice and, obviously, it was necessary to share it with him."

THE UNBELIEVING VETERINARY

Account of Omarov Ramazan, 37, Lakh, director of the veterinarian and zootechnical station of the Tliarata district, Republic of Daghestan.

"On the 20 August 1959, I was returning across the mountain to Antzug. It was close to 6 o'clock in the evening. The visibility was very good. I was descending a small valley where trees were rare.

When I reached the big white stone . . . I noticed an animal moving around below. I thought it was a bear, and hid behind a bush. I had no weapon on me. I had only my bridle and the bag in which I transport the vaccination equipment. Hidden behind the bush, I began to make observations. The animal, which originally appeared to have been sitting, suddenly stood up and headed in my direction on two legs. It was a creature which resembled both a man and an ape at the same time. From my childhood, I had heard accounts of the kaptars, but I didn't believe in them. Well, this was what I was now seeing with my own eyes.

Its body hair was long and black, like a goat's. The neck was essentially nonexistent; the head rested directly on the shoulders. Long hair hung down from the head. The kaptar was coming closer. It was heading, not so much towards me, but to the side. It was a male. The head was long, pointing upwards, conical, ovoid in shape. The long arms hung almost to the knees. He was walking along, and they were tossing around, as if articulated with screws; they gave the impression of being mounted on the joints, like a child's toy.

About 200 yards from me, this strange creature crossed the path and sat down again. It rested sitting down for two or three minutes, the hands touching the ground. It made one think of a sportsman who was doing physical exercises. Then, he got up again, and headed towards a shrub on the other side of the crest, and disappeared. I did not see it again. I abandoned my bush and quietly returned home.

What struck me again? It climbed the slope very fast, making strides of a metre or even more. A man could not climb a steep slope making such big strides.

I think of a chimpanzee which I have seen at the zoo in Tbilisi. The hair of the chimpanzee is shorter, the head rounder. The arms and legs are also shorter. It must be said, it is true, that its height is also shorter. The kaptar did not measure less than 1.80 m [5 ft 11 in] and it resembled a man more than an ape. It walked upright, its head just inclined a little more forward on its shoulders. No tail. Another typical thing: in the wolf or bear, one always sees the ears, even though they are short, whereas in this case, the head hair covered the ears, and they were not visible. Obviously, I was scared. But, my curiosity was still stronger than my fear. I have lived 37 years and I used to think that the kaptar was the invention of superstitious people. Well, that has been proved false; I saw it myself."

THE ALMASTY HUNT

Account of Efendiev Mustapha Abdul, 61, Lesge, schoolmaster, Makhachkala, in the Republic of Daghestan.

"My neighbour, an old shepherd with 90 years of experiences, Musa Idrissov, had this adventure: in the autumn of 1955, the shepherds of the village of Knor were driving their flocks of sheep, as they did every year, to the winter pastures by passing over the mountains into Azerbaijan. They had to cross the Saryzh forest and halt for the night. The shepherds slaughtered a goat, lit a wood fire and began to prepare supper. Towards midnight, when they were settling down to eat, they heard noisy breathing ... and noticed a creature of human appearance, covered with black hair. Its appearance had not been provoked by jostling among the sheep... the shepherds took fright. 'It's an alnab,' said Musa. 'It is probably hungry, and wants us to give it something to eat.' Taking some bread, and a morsel of grilled meat, he threw them at the alnab. The latter hurled itself greedily onto the food, and quickly devoured it. Then, after having remained on the spot a certain moment, it backed up and disappeared. In the darkness, its eyes shone like a cat's.

Fearing an attack by this being which the shepherds, the Lesges, knew poorly or not at all, they climbed into the trees, rifles in their hands. Effectively, at the end of about an hour and a half, the alnab reappeared and attempted to possess itself of the meat. At that moment, Musa fired. They heard a horrible howling. The alnab let go of the meat and turned to the side of the detonation. Then, it was the turn of Daud to fire. The alnab made haste to disappear, limping.

At dawn, the shepherds noticed traces of blood on the grass. Musa and Daud took to the trail; the third shepherd remained with the sheep. The trail led Musa and Daud to Pchar. There, on the river bank, they found the bloody corpse of the alnab. One bullet had hit it in the leg, the other had pierced its chest.

It was 2 metres [6ft 7 in] tall. Its head was shaped like an egg. The nose was like sunken into the face. A very massive chin. Long tangled hair hung from its head. From its body issued an strong, very repulsive odour.

The shepherds told themselves that nobody would believe them, and that it would be necessary to take away some evidence. They sliced off the ears and a handful of hair from the head; and from the right hand, the thumb and index finger.

When Musa and Daud regained their camp, the newly arrived shepherds were already waiting for them. As they had foreseen, the latter did not believe them. They were not even convinced by their physical evidence. Then, Musa and Daud led them to the river where the corpse lay.

Three months later, Musa returned to the village and started to build himself a house. He buried the ears, hair, and fingers of the alnab under the foundation as a talisman title preserving the alnabs.

This is the moment when he will show them to me."

AGILE AND BOUNDING

Account of Lobtanidze B.F., Georgian, engineer at Tbilisi in the Republic of Georgia. Letter addressed to the Museum of Anthropology at the University of Moscow, 16 December 1960.

"After having read in *Tbilisi Evening* your article, 'Is there a snowman in the Transcaucasus', I have decided to write to you in order to recount an episode that I experienced some years ago.

It was in the summer of 1946. We were with my brother, R.I. Metreveli, now assistant of the Academy of Arts in Georgia, in the village of Orjonikidze in the district of Lagodekhi. One day we undertook to go haying, three or four kilometres from the village, in the tobacco plantations. A little boy from our family, A.F. Lobtanidze, accompanied us.

We were just preparing to go back, when the child cried out: 'Look, look, someone is observing us from the tree.' We fixed our gaze attentively on the tree and discovered a man who, shielding his eyes with his hand, was looking in our direction. However, he did not seem to have discovered us and we remained quiet, and decided to observe him. Soon, nevertheless, we changed our intention. Indeed, this creature began to leap from one branch to the other, up and down, down and up, and this with such speed that we decided it was an ape. Feeling more confident, we approached to some 25 to 30 yards, but there, we were seized by genuine fear.

It was something frightening. Neither man nor ape. It resembled rather a man of enormous height, with long hair covering the whole of its body. Finally, it hung from a branch with its hands, and leaped onto the ground from a height for about 4 metres [13 feet] and disappeared into the bushes.

Some minutes later, we heard footsteps and the sound of conversation, and three men from the neighbouring village made their appearance on the road. Well, the tree where this creature had been was quite close to the road.

I swear we were all very scared. Returning to the village, we recounted our adventure. Certain people laughed, others shared our sentiments.

[At this point, the editor appears to have left out a section of Koffmann's article by mistake, because the text continues, without any break, with the questioning of someone called Kapanadze, not previously mentioned. I have translated it for the sake of completeness.]

Why didn't Apakidze tell exactly the same thing as you?(Up to this point, Kapanadze was not aware that I had just seen his old companion, in a distant village, from which I had arrived directly by car.)

"Because he was sleeping. It was I who woke up. As long as the wild man was coming down and drinking, I did not dare move. When it started to get up, I hastily jostled Apakidze and said to him: 'Look quickly, what is that – a bear or what?' The old man whispered: 'Be quiet, be quiet, I know what it is.'

He could not tell you everything, as he had seen it only from the moment the wild man got up."

Do you believe that the wild man saw you?

I think so. It would not have been able to not see us. Firstly, it was coming down facing our cabin, and me. Secondly, the wood fire was burning, since he was preparing breakfast. It could not have missed seeing the fire. Also, when it had drunk and stood up again, before commencing to go back up, it turned its head towards us, glanced at us over its shoulder, and went away.

It did not resemble the imprint of a bear at all. It was a human imprint, but larger. The heel was wider than a man's and, at the base of the toes, the sole of the foot was very much wider."

These illustrations, unrelated to any specific account, are taken from photocopies. I apologize for the poor quality. This first one was captioned:

"*Figure 1.*Imprint of a foot whose provenance is the Ala Tau mountains of Soviet Asia: a size 42 shoe came up to the level of the little toe."

[Note: Ala Tau is the name of a number of ranges in Kazakhstan, Kyrgyrstan, and Uzbekistan, some of which belong to the North Tien Shan. This is a *long* way from the Caucasus, and a reminder that similar creatures have been reported all across central Asia. Note also that French size 42 = size 8½ British and size 9 U.S. length 235-238 mm or 9.3 in. The same photograph was published in *Year of the Sasquatch* by John Green (1970) courtesy of Prof. B. F. Porshnev, and said to have been taken in the Tien Shan in 1962. The photograph was claimed to be life size, and the heel to little toe measurement really was 9.3 in., and the total length about 14½ in. Dr. John Napier, who was one of the world's leading primatologists, estimated the heights of bigfoots by multiplying foot length by a factor of 6.6. Yes, we know that people of the same height can have different sized shoes, but he was able to show that it is a good estimate of height to within a few inches, which is all that matters. In that case, the above footprint indicates a height of 8 feet.]

This footprint really did come from the Caucasus ie from Kabardino- Balkaria. The caption was: "*Figure 2*. Imprint of an almasty foot (the track amounted to a score) removed entire after consolidation of the soil. Valley of the Malka. March 1978."

DESCRIPTIVE MEMO ON THE ALMASTY

The number of citations is limited; they could be multiplied by dozens. The citations are accompanied by a figure (the reference number of the file) and a letter designating the republic ("a" for Azerbaijan, "g" for Georgia, "k" for Karbarda, Balkaria, Karachai, etc).

The sexual appurtenance of the beings observed is designated by the usual symbols. When it was not determined, which was frequently the case, the individual is indicated by "x". The children and adolescents figure under the symbol Δ.

The anatomic characteristics are presented according to the descriptive scheme generally admitted by anthropometry: height, skin and its derivatives, limbs and their proportions, skull.

HEIGHT

The height varies according to the age of the individual. Its seems, however, in the aggregate, to reach or surpass the human average. Individuals of 2m – 2.20 m [6ft 7 in to 7ft 3 in] are not rare.

One thing is certain: there is no sexual dimorphism with respect to height, the large adult females are as tall and as powerful as the males.

THE SKIN AND ITS DERIVITIVES

Colour:

"There, where there is no hair, the skin is black" (Δ 52 k).

"The skin of the face is black" (♀ 54 k).

"The skin of the palm of the hands is dark brown ... On the buttocks, hair is absent, the skin is dark brown" (x 141 k).

Hairy Coat

"It seemed to me that the chest is hairier than the back. On the buttocks, the hairs are much rarefied and shorter, you can see dark skin through it. At the level of the kidneys, the hair is very thick and very long, partially covering the top of the buttocks. On the shoulders, it is so thick that is is impossible to distinguish where it ends and the hair of the head commences[13]. The legs and the back of the feet are covered with what appears to be very coarse hair" (♂ 47 a).

"The back of the hand has very little hair, but on the forearm, it is so long that it covers the back of the hand" (x 126 k).

This hairy coat is absent from the hand at birth, as two observations testify. Nevertheless, it is rapidly installed:

"In a corner of the cabin, on the hay, a [female] almasty was seated; she held in her arms a quite small ... the infant had black skin, entirely covered with black hair, but short and not thick" (♀ Δ 1 ak).

---

[13] In this, and every other passage, it is important to note that French has separate words for body hair and head hair.

Head Hair:
Very abundant, long, very coarse ("like a horse's mane" 7 a). That of the males reach "just to the shoulder blades, even a little lower" (♂ 1 a). It is much longer in the females:

"... very long hair, to the waist or lower" (71 k).

"... then, she got up slowly, collected her long hair which came down to below the waist and threw it over her left forearm" (49 k).

Odour:
It has been mentioned in several of the testimonies cited. The observers are not short of expressions:

"... it stinks like a ruptured dog" (♂ 76 k).

"... it stinks like a latrine ditch. There, where it was sitting its odour remained for a week" (♂ 100 k).

It appears to me that this powerful odour is principally emitted by the male: every time it is raised, it involves "men" ie individuals whose sexual appurtenance could not be established precisely, but which certainly seemed to be males. No description of a female is accompanied by this detail:

"I did not notice any odour" (♀ 60 k: the witness being only a metre away).

Nails:
"The fingernails were very long" (x 38 a).

"The nails of the hands are broad, just as broad as a human's. But long. They are not narrowed on both sides and hooked, like the claws of a bear. They are broad, straight, and long" (♂ 47 a).

"On the toes, the nails are flat, longer than a man's, but a little deformed and hooked, like the hooves of poorly tended sheep" (x k).

BREASTS
They are described in the testimonies cited. Some precise references:

"...She measured 1.50m – 1.60 m [5 ft - 5 ft 3 in] ... Probably still young: her breasts were like those of a little girl" (35 k).

"She had very long breasts ... At that moment, she turned to the side and threw a breast over her shoulder" (26 k).

"Her breasts were very long. They were both thrown over her shoulders" (72 k).

"Long, half-empty breasts hung down on her belly. It was as if someone had deposited something, a bit of grain, for example, or a small melon, at the bottom of a long, empty bag, and hung it up. This was the way her breast hung" (48 k).

UPPER LIMBS
"The shoulders are carried forward" (♂ 49 k).
"Hunched, the shoulders abandoned towards the front, arms longer than a man's" (♀ 48 k).
"Its arms, longer than a man's, reached its knees. They were held away form the body and slightly flexed at the shoulders" (Δ 31 k).
"Its arm is big, like a man's thigh" (♀ ΔΔ 86 k).
"The *hand* resembles a man's, only there was no flesh there (the witness pointed to the thenar pad which is situated on the palm at the base of the thumb), the palm is flat. The thumb is short, shorter than the other fingers in comparison to a man's. The other fingers, on the contrary, are longer. The thumb is not positioned as in a man's, opposite the other fingers, but on the same level as them. The nails are long, but not pointed. The palm is covered in black callosities" (Δ 52 k).

LOWER LIMBS
"Her shoulders are broad, but her pelvis narrow" (♀ 54 k).
"The legs are short and arched" (♀ Mashk. 1 k).
"The thighs are stronger than in a man" (x 40 a).
"The thighs are big, the leg is very thin" (♀ 141 k).
"The legs are the same thickness as a man's forearm above the wrist" (x 38 a).
"... The feet are directed inwards, the knees a little bent, the legs bowed like those of a good horseman" (x 31 k).
"... legs bowed, feet directed inwards" (x 64 a).
"... the legs, she held them like this" (the witness spread the legs, knees lightly bent, feet directed inwards)" (♀ 119 k).
"The legs are thin, but the feet are big" (Δ 103 k).
"The feet are thick" (♀ Δ 60 a).
"The feet are slightly bent inwards. The toes are spread out like a fan" (x 31 k).
"The feet are very broad; less at the heel, but towards the base of the toes, the foot widens and at this spot (the witness indicates the first metatarso-phalangeal joint) it is as big as an ox's (x 107 k).

SKULL

General configuration and relationship between the cerebral and facial skull

"... While she herself was tall and robust, her skull was small, narrow, and shaped like an egg" (♀ 54 k).

"The skull is not very high, but flatter than in a human ... There is also something curious: in a man, the face is narrow and smaller in relation to the skull. However, with it, the perimeter of the skull is convenient. This made it a very large face, a true maw" (x 31 k).

"The face is not good. Like in a man, but the mouth is carried forward.

Question: As in a monkey?[14].

Reply: Why a monkey? I have seen monkeys. The maw of a monkey, it is stretched out in front, like that of a dog. With him, the maw is less stretched out than in a monkey, but more than in a man. His face, it is sort of half-way between a monkey's and a man's" (♂ 13 a).

"The *forehead* is narrow, sloping backwards."

"The forehead is low" (♀ Δ 34 k).

"The forehead is narrow" (♂ 79 k).

Brow Ridge. Described as very projecting by several of the witnesses cited. Some other descriptions:

"The brow overhangs the eyes, like a helmet visor" (♀ 141 k)

"The eyebrows are extremely projecting" (Δ of 4-5 years, 52 k)

Cheek bones. Their strong prominence is also often mentioned in the communications presented here. It is a trait which figures in almost all the descriptions of the face.

CHIN

"Its chin was not like a man's. A man has a fine, pointed chin; its chin was round, heavy, not pointed, but massive" (x 31 k).

"The chin is not like a person's: it is not there: (the witness indicated the prominence of the chin) (♂ 100 k).

NOSE

"The nose is like that of a syphilitic. That spot (the witness indicated the root of the nose) is not there."

---

[14] The French word can mean both "ape" and "monkey". The latter is probably intended here.

"The nose is like that of someone who is sticking his face forcefully against a pane of glass."

"The nose is small, flattened, as if someone had forcefully crushed it against the face" (♂ 76 k).

"The nose is very broad and flattened, the nostrils gaping at the front like 10 kopek coins" (♀ 119 k).

EARS

"The ears are flat and are situated higher than in a man" (Δ 52 k).

"His face is like a man's. Only the ears are stretched out higher" (♀ 43 a).

"If there is anything which distinguishes it from a man, it is certainly the ears: the ears are big, bigger than a man's" (♂ 126 k).

MOUTH, LIPS

"The mouth is widely split" (Δ 31 k).

"The mouth is widely split" (♀ 60 k).

"The mouth is twice as big as ours" (♂ 20 a).

"The lips are thin like those of an ape" (♀ 71 k).

TEETH

"The teeth are strong" (♂ 21 a).

"The teeth are stronger than in a man" (♀ 65 a).

"The teeth are remarkable. It happens among people that one tooth may be longer, another shorter. With it, they are certainly regular and white, white. Like those of a man. I saw them well the second time, while I was perched in the tree" (♂ 47 a).

"... It stood upright, in the light of the headlights, lips curled back, and I saw the teeth well, notably, two large canines, but I can no longer recall whether they were upper or lower" (♂ 22 a).

"I opened its mouth with the handle of my whip ... Still quite young, but already large canines, like a dog, large and pointed, but yellow. The upper and lower canines intersected, as in a dog" (Δ of 4-5 years, 52 k).

"The teeth are as in a man, but stronger. The four front teeth are very big" (♀ 119 k).

EYE

"The eyes are elongated and oblique, as in the Chinese, but still stronger" (♂ 4 ak).

"The eyes are strongly bridled, red, not good" (x 67 k).

"... the eyes red, bridled ..." (♀ 68 k).

"What I especially retained were the eyes, oblique and red. With dogs, the eyes sometimes shine very strongly at night. Well, with it, there was the same thing, only red" (x 62 k).

"Its eyes shone in the darkness like two cigarettes" (x, Karachai).

"I was quite close to it. Its eyes were lightly reflecting with a reddish glow. I started to slowly back up. When I was at the side, the eyes almost did not shine; when I had backed up, they were shining with a powerful red glow" (x 28 k).

"When I saw her for the first time (night), the eyes flashed at moments with a vivid red colour. I at first believed that they were cigarettes and it said to myself: "Hold on! They are smoking like us." The second time also, their eyes sometimes glowed with a red light. But not all the time. That probably depends on the illumination" (♂♀ 49 k).

NECK

"The neck, it is like it isn't there. The head is placed directly on the shoulders" (♂♀ 17 a).

"The head is pushed down directly into the shoulders" (♂ 142 k).

PORTRAIT OF THE ALMASTY

The almasty of the Caucasus thus appears as a bipedal being, with a vertical stature, and quasi human demeanour, whose height, variable according to age, reaches 1.80 m to 2.20 m in the adults of both sexes; it has a robust constitution and a very powerful musculature.

Its very dark skin is covered with a pelt of long (15 cm/6 in), coarse hair whose thickness and colour (generally reddish, more rarely black or grey) varies according to age, the anatomic region, and the individual. The skin of the newborns is pink and glabrous.

The hair of the head is abundant in both sexes. The long, pendulous breasts of the females can be thrown over the back.

The back is hunched, the neck is not apparent.

The upper limbs are long; the hand is furnished with long, powerful fingers with long, flat nails. The muscles of the shoulders and arms are extremely well developed.

The lower limbs, on the contrary, are rather short, especially the leg which is, moreover, slightly bowed; the foot is flat, relatively short, very broad, with long, strong toes, which are very mobile in the sagittal and horizontal planes.

The skull is small and ovoid; the forehead is low, narrow, and retreating; the cranium is flat with a prominent supra-orbital ridge; the zygomatic arches jut forward a lot; the prognathism is important (? oncognathism); the massive, round mandible possesses a powerful set of teeth with developed canines; the root of the nose is sunken, the nose is broad and flattened with flaring nostrils; the ocular slits are very oblique, the dark, reddish eyes project a red glow at night; the mouth is broadly split with the lips thin and extended.

The strong and repugnant odour which issues from the almasty may simply be due to a filthy pelt.

Such are, transferred into professional language, the essential morphological characteristics of the individual which the inhabitants of the Caucasus describe.

EXACTITUDE AND COHERENCE OF THE DESCRIPTIONS

The anatomic authenticity of these characteristics is imposing. To cite only the skull, for example, all the descriptions collected constitute so many precise and very evocative anatomic symptoms.

The harmony of the ensemble of these symptoms is equally striking. Not only is each of the traits described by the witnesses exact in itself but, in addition, its presence is supported by other elements, themselves also present and authentic. Bourrelet supra-orbital, root of the nose retreating, epicanthus, prognathism, playrhiny (wide nostrils) etc, mutually introduce into the framework of known and precise correlations. Even the absence of certain traits like the chin eminence, for example, is logical: an attribute exclusive to man, *Homo sapiens sapiens*, it was a non issue on this skull. Reconstructed uniquely from oral testimonies, the skull of the almasty thus appears a coherent entity.

With regard to the other parts of the body, the some conclusions prevail.

The necessity of balancing the weight of the massive, heavy face of a small skull (with the *foramen magnum* perhaps pointing backwards) crowning a spinal column held in a stooped posture, also with a rounding of the shoulder girdle to which attaches the heavy upper limbs ("its arm had the same diameter as a man's thigh") requires such an important cervical and scapular musculature that the column retreats into the neck and is practically nonexistent.

The thickness of the thigh associated with the thinness of the calf is also explained. The thigh muscles are frequently called to hold the lower limbs in slight flexure, a posture perhaps serving to moderate the considerable body weight and permitting silent travel in the woody, rocky habitat. Let us remember what the Georgian woodcutter attempted to explain: "its gait is human, but it walks a little like an animal".

The weak volume of the posterior muscles of the leg, without doubt unexpected in a subject so perfectly bipedal, could be explained by a structure of the plantar skeleton, precisely adapted to the necessity of raising an enormous weight. This is suggested by the length, unusual in a human, of the calcaneum. The talo-crural is then seen to have been moved back distally, with the increase in the length of the arms of the tarsal lever, and respectively, the shortening of the metatarsal lever. Under these conditions, the requirement of bending the foot is singularly lessened. This relationship of forces has been described in the perfectly intact skeleton of the Neanderthal foot of Kiik-Koba (the celebrated site of the Crimea where there was recovered a Neanderthal skeleton in which the two feet were preserved practically in their totality: 52 elements out of 54). The same relationship of forces is suspected by the American scholar Grover S. Krantz in the foot of the Sasquatch of the Rockies, first cousin to the almasty. We also find it in certain negroid ethnic groups, presenting an astonishing thinness of the calf muscle (triceps surae): it precisely involves particularly fast and agile hunters.

The colour of the almasty's eyes is nothing extraplanetary. It is easily understood if one remembers that twilight vision, assured by the vivid red visual purple of the rods, is reinforced in certain nocturnal species by a special structure, the tapetum. The crystals of this structure, like thousands of bits of ice, direct into the owner's retina the weak rays of light which have penetrated into the eye. The colour of this piercing metallic glow which fascinate us in our domestic animals, depends on that at the base of the eye, which is not the same in all species, and varies according to the structure of the ocular envelopes: yellow in the elephant and other species, and green in the canids, it is red in the primates, including man. This last, unlike those monkeys whose visual acuity, notably at night, is much superior to our own, possess few rods and his tapetum is almost nonexistent. But just the same, a powerful glow, even in the human eye, produces this reddish reflection which one often notices on photographs taken with a flash. The vivid red glow of the almasty's eye, a detail at first sight unusual and disconcerting, is found to have a banal physiological explanation.

Another conclusion of course appears: the adequacy of the anatomic form to its function. This adequacy is so perfect that, knowing one, it becomes possible to not only explain, but to present the other.

The absence of the thenar pad (the part of the palm of the hand situated at the base of the thumb), mentioned by several witnesses, indicates a weak opposability of the thumb. Effectively, the witnesses have observed that the almasty grasps objects by unilateral prehension of the five fingers.

In the same way, given the setting of the head, riveted to the shoulders by powerful muscles, one can expect ease of movements: in order to look to the side, the almasty pivots its shoulders and the upper part of the trunk, "like a wolf" the witnesses say, and it in fact turns around in the same manner. The almasty also uses its head as a means of combat, butting head down, like a ram: "the almasty hits with its head". The wide, flaring nostrils let us predict a highly developed sense of smell. It is observed that the almasty uses its sense of smell often; it follows a track, frequently leaning over, without breaking its pace to smell the ground.

GREAT APE OR LATE NEANDERTHAL?

All this information is found confirmed by certain documents.

The skeleton of the hand corresponds to the skeleton of the mummified hand of Pangboche, attributed by the lamas of Tibet to the yeti, described by numerous specialists as belonging to a primate, and uniting human and ape characteristics..

The foot which the witnesses describe: massive, splayed, with a broad heel and powerful, mobile toes, with the characteristic inflexion of its distal portion ("inner foot"), corresponds precisely to the the footprints which I have been able to photograph and collect in the form of moulds in the uninhabited regions of the mountain.

The almasty lays out for itself, under rocky shelters or in caves, bedding manufactured from grasses especially chosen by itself (and not, importantly, with just that material it finds at hand, as does the bear, for example). The provisions or the remains of food left on this bedding confirms the alimentary list given by the people of the country.

Hairy hominoid creatures whose eyes throw a red light, described by scholars of North America, called "Sasquatches" by the Indians and Bigfoot by the whites, are not without kinship with the almasty. The hundreds of descriptions furnished by the inhabitants of the Caucasus correspond in every case with those of three Russian scholars who have opened the Caucasian chapter: Prof. C. Satunin in1899, Dr. V. Karapetian in 1941, and Inspector K. Leontiev in 1958.

Extrapolating hundreds of testimonies, submitted to a statistical analysis and an anatomic scrutiny, the information concerning the morphology, ecology, and ethnology of the almasty, constitute authentic landmarks and summary whose convergence raises the appearance of an personage which is anatomically concrete, well defined, balanced, viable, and destitute of all whimsical elements. The morphological reality, the biological truth, the anthropological authenticity of this individual is indisputable.

Furthermore, the criteria which the characteristics raise of a science, human paleontology, of which the old Caucasian shepherds, for the most part illiterate, are ignorant is of course, obvious. The almasty described by them with the precision and realism of men in constant contact with nature cannot be the fruit of the imagination.

What then is the almasty? Great ape for some, late Neanderthal for others, notably Prof Porshnev, the almasty certainly presents more hominid than simian traits: the absence of sexual dimorphism in height and robust constitution, long breasts in the females, abundant head hair, and the foot, are characteristics of the species, *Homo*. The canines (often described by the observers as protruding and analogous to those of a dog) bring to this picture an importunate but important note.

The antero-posterior lengthening of the skull, the lowering of he cranial vault, the prominence of the superciliary and zygomatic arches, the breadth of the face, the heavy, rounded mandible lacking a chin, the hunched back, the breadth of the shoulders, that of the hand, the length of the fingers, the weakness of the thumb, the shortness of the leg in respect to the thigh, the massiveness of the foot, all those anatomic traits associated with undoubtedly human criteria, evoke the Neanderthal or rather the paleanthropes.[15] The elevated height of the almasty is found in fossil Palestinian men close to the Neanderthals (Skhul IV and V) and in

---

[15] "Paléanthropien" has no equivalent in English. In Koffmann's lexicon (omitted for simplicity) it was defined as the stage between *Homo erectus* and the Neanderthals.

the Neanderthals of Shanidar in Kurdistan, in Iraq, thus in regions relatively close to the Caucasus.

It would seem then that the fossil species of the Caucasus may belong to the human tribe, perhaps of a parallel, neighbouring lineage. However, in the current stage of research, respect for scientific rigour does not permit one to establish a diagnosis. Is it necessary to insist on the repercussions which the discovery and study of the almasty would have on the human sciences?

. . . .

Here is how Professor Piveteau, member of the Academy of Sciences, honorary professor at the College of France, qualifies the almasty, in some Reflexions on this Hominid of the Caucasus, addressed to Dr M.-J. Koffmann in 1987, and which we publish here.

The concordance of the testimonies collected by Dr Marie-Jeanne Koffmann, and the fact that they stem from different and unequal sorts of cultures, plead in favour of their truthfulness. Indeed, one does not see in them the expression of ideologies or of scientific preconceptions, but the translation of naive observations, simply expressing what has been seen. The existence of the singular being thus described therefore does not appear contestable.

If one cannot claim to give a precise description of them, it is possible to establish some essential features and one is there is a big quandary as to placing it in the framework of classic systematics. It is assuredly a Primate, and its bipedalism serves to rank it is the lineage of the Hominidae, that is to say, in the lineage whose final end is man.

This bipedalism does not involve, according to the different testimonies, a gait similar to man's, but rather evokes that of the Australopithecines, hominids which are not human. On the other hand, the great length of the arms may be considered an archaic attribute, that is to say, prehuman. Thus, by their carriage, the hominids of the Caucasus would have scarcely reached the human stage.

But how will the paleontologist, from whose point of view we place ourselves here, see the hominid become human?

In such research, the anatomic criterion has its importance. However the psychic criterion appears to us to be preponderant.

Reflection, language, society, such are the essential characteristics of man.

Seen from outside, reflective thought is attested by tool-making, the result of intentional work.

Is the hominid of the Caucasus capable of making tools? Nothing in the observations reported up to now seem to permit us to affirm it. An in-depth study of the habitation sites would thus be necessary.

Does it possess an articulated language? Indications are only of simple vocalisations, never of true language.

On the other hand, it does seem nevertheless to have a social organisation, at least certain modes of grouping.

If the authenticity of the hominid of the Caucasus is definitely established, we find ourselves in the presence of a creature in which there seems to link the animal and the human. On its exact nature, that is to say, its place in human evolution, we can make some hypotheses.

It evokes the myth of the wild man, which has not ceased to haunted the mind. It again presents itself, in the age of enlightenment, by a hairy body and a mixture of animal and human traits, showing somewhat indistinctly the boundaries of human nature. In our current scientific paradigm,we will be able to consider it as being a check on humanisation, like an degraded being which has lost the most characteristic attributes of the normal man. But one should not forget that nature is more fecund and richer than our imagination.

These vain hypotheses must give place to a genuine scientific study, and no-one would appear to be better than qualified to undertake it and lead it than Dr M.-J. Koffmann. I strongly wish, and I am assured, that it is the vow of the French scientific community, that Mrs Koffmann could obtain all the means that will permit her to bring light on the strange and exciting problem rising from the enigmatic being of the Caucasus.

Paris, 10 June 1987

Jean Piveteau
Member of the Academy of Sciences
Member of the Royal Academy of Belgium

REPLY BY DR M.-J. KOFFMANN

I was struck, for example, by your remarks that the almasty's bipedalism "does not involve . . . a gait similar to man's, but rather evokes that of the Australopithecines".

Now, in the few testimonies which you have (thirteen out of hundreds!), it is only a question of a calm gait, which already differs slightly from that of a man. I have never been able to put in writing the carriage of the almasty running, except the unanimous affirmation that it is extremely rapid; my informants, even the most cultivated, have always been totally incapable of describing the run to me. Their confused explanations are no more intelligible than their clumsy attempts to imitate this manner of projecting itself forward by powerful leaps. I think of this Russian engineer, surprising in his car, in full daylight, an almasty on a narrow mountain detour trail, where it was trapped between two walls, and keeping it, at 40 kph [25 mph], at the level of the right headlight for more than 400 metres when the creature was at last able to jump through a break into the forest. An experienced observer of nature and animals, with diplomas from two superior schools, he still did not know how to explain the manner of running of this being, which he watched carefully at 2 metres' distance; he saw the muscles of the thigh rippling under the fur – the creature emanated an impression of prodigious strength. Like the other witnesses, this educated man noted that the run was effectively by bounds, but he was not able to give me a picture, neither by imitation ("they were not by movements accessible to a human being") nor, especially, in writing, as I begged him.

Tools. Apart from the use of stones, which they throw with great precision, I have no information on tool-making, except the description of a sort of club found, along with alimentary rubbish, next to some bedding, in a cave, and definitely belonging to an almasty: the two hunters, having quickly left the site, and hiding on the opposite slope, soon saw the the owner return home. "The handle of the club was chewed with the teeth so as to make it comfortable to hold in the hand." It is hardly necessary, however, to seek out a hominid for this exploit – the smallest chimpanzee knows how to do better.

On the contrary, the almasty knows how to reanimate and preserve a dying wood fire left by shepherds. My data on these facts are absolutely certain, for it is easy to understand my stupefaction and emotion when, quite indifferently, it was recounted for the first time and the scrupulous prudence that I committed to assure myself of their reality.

The "social" groups were, not long ago, very important numerically, forming sorts of bands. Let us not forget that today we are present, alas, at the end of the species, whose last few representatives are wandering, solitary, among the debris of their former area of habitation. Perhaps the situation is not, in other regions of the globe, as tragic as in the Caucasus, but everywhere the reduction in numbers is evident.

. . . .

Eminent anthropologist, author of numerous works on human evolution, Professor Piveteau recently died. His pupils and disciples, who were always impressed by the extent of his knowledge and his remarkable mind for synthesis, all those who knew him, retain of him the picture of a modest, generous scholar, always in quest of a truth very difficult to grasp when it came to the origins of man.

Chapter 3

The Mongolian Wild Man's Last Stand

In 1962 the International Committee for the Study of Human-like Hairy Bipeds was formed, and for the next few years they published articles in *Genus*, a peer-reviewed journal of demography centred in Rome, but which nevertheless published articles in several different languages. Fortunately, too, all the issues are now online in the digital library, JSTOR[16]. A number of articles in this book are translations from that journal.

One reason for taking cryptozoology seriously is the possibility that a significant species is going extinct before science has even established its existence. Thus, throughout the boreal forests of Russia, as far as Siberia, legends abound of primates apparently similar to the North American bigfoot. However, if the legends are correct, a wide tract of Central Asia also harbours isolated pockets of a different type of primate: slightly smaller, slightly more social, slightly more manlike (but only slightly). Such, for example, are the almasties of the Caucasus, and possibly the barmanu of Chitral. Peasants still claim to see them in Tajikistan. In Mongolia the term is *almas* (singular; it is not the plural of "alma"), and the leading researcher used to be Professor Yöngsiyebü-Biambyn Rinchen of Ulaan Baatar (1905 - 1977). The Mongolian alphabets are different to ours, so his surname has also been transliterated as "Rincen" and "Rinčen", and his initial as "P" and "B"

In any case, in 1964 Prof Rinchen wrote a paper for journal, *Genus* in which he claimed that almas were then restricted to an area of 1,000 square kilometres [380 square miles] in his country.

Rincen, Prof. P. R. (1964) Almas still exist in Mongolia. *Genus* 20: 186 – 192

The first few pages are concerned mostly with philology. We learn that, as I had originally suspected, nearly all the etymologies given in Ivan T. Sanderson's *Abominable Snowmen* are ridiculous. The origin of the word, "almas" is unknown, although it does

---

16

https://www.jstor.org/journal/genus#:~:text=GENUS%20is%20an%20online%20and,interdisciplinary%20approach%20to%20population%20studies.

contribute to quite a few place names, such as Almasyn Ulan Oula, the Red Mountains of Almases.

However, I intend to start at the last line on page 189, where the eye-witness accounts begin. This is not a translation; the paper is in English. Nevertheless, since English remained a second language for both the author and the editors, I have taken the liberty of smoothing out the text in a few places. Even so, some phrases are difficult to understand.

. . . .

I had collected information about Almases since 1927 and lost some chances of obtaining at least four corpses of Almases on account of rank ignorance of time-serving persons who were to equip an expedition.

During these 37 years the numerous information at my disposal show an area of Almas habitation to be constantly shrinking. Development of air and automobile transport, of virgin and unused desert lands, increase in hunting and improvement of hunters' fire-arms changed the habitual area of wild animals of great deserts and steppes.

The "iron curtain" of the Transmongolian railway now divided the wasteland of their habitation into "Western" and "Eastern" Gobi and, for example, the Gobi antelopes dare not now cross a strange reeking and repugnant steel snake with its constantly ringing and whistling wire of telegraph posts.

The wild horses and camels and Almases retired to the West and during the last forty years the area of habitation of Almases has been very reduced. At present it is limited by [?to] the woodless mountainous region of about one thousand square kilometres on the junction of Kobdo [now Khovd] and Bayan-olegei [Bayan-Ölgii] provinces. This very rugged wasteland rich in edible roots and berries, mouflons and chamoises is now the last refuge of Almases in Mongolia.

After many attempts I had succeeded in sending in autumn 1962 Mr. Damdin, one of the workers of our State Museum, to make reconnaissances in this region and he returned back in December with a lot of very interesting information, which permitted me and him to organize his second trip in autumn 1963.

According to the data presented in the reports of Mr. Damdin, now retired 64 years old pensioner, who is preparing for his third trip to the Land of Almases, there are many eyewitnesses who met an Almas during these last three years, including August 1963.

Among these eyewitnesses there are simple hunters and cattle breeders, members of peasant cooperatives, men and women, students and teachers, former soldiers and officers of the Army etc.

As a result of Mr. Damlin's first trip, we have now at our disposal a skull of an Almas[17] found near the Red Mountains of Almases in the district Bulgan somon Kodbo province. [A somon is a district.]

Mr. Choijoa, Mongol Torgut native of Sinkiang [Xinjiang], former cattle breeder and subsequently a worker of the Fruit-Growing Experimental Station of the Mongolian Academy of Bulgan somo told a story of this great find:

- It happened at about ten o'clock on 26th June 1953. I remember the time, day, and month because this event had utterly surprised me and was engraved on my heart.

At dawn of that day I went to search for my lost camels in the direction of the so-called Red Mountain of Almases. It was a beautiful sunny morning when I dropped into the ravines. The wind spread a fragrance of highland flowers and herbs but I was in a hurry to leave before the midday heat this labyrinth of canyons and ravines. My camel climbed up and down in the craggy defiles. Suddenly I saw in the corner of a secluded ravine under two small ammodendron bushes[18] something of a camel colour. I approached and saw a hairy corpse of a robust humanlike creature dried and half buried in the sand. I had never seen such a humanlike being covered by camel-coloured, brownish-yellow short hairs and I recoiled, although in my native land of Sinkiang I had seen many dead men killed in battle. But who was this strange dead thing - man or beast? I decided to return back and thoroughly examine it. I approached once more and looked down from my camel. The dead thing was not a bear or ape and the same time it was not a man like a Mongol, Kazakh, Chinese, or Russian. The hair of its head was longer than on its body [19]. The skin on the groin and armpits wad darkened and shrivelled like a hide of a dead camel.

I have also examined the terrain near this body and found any rests of wears.[20]. Fear seized my heart. I remembered the old tales of Vetala vampires and thought I was seeing one of them before me. And I hurried away. After my return home I informed our local administration and

---

[17] But see note.

[18] saxsaul, *Haloxylon ammodendron*

[19] similar to the almasties of the Caucasus

[20] Presumably he means he found no remains of clothing.

Mr. Chimeddorje, manager of the Fruit-growing Station, but no-one took any notice of my account. And only after ten years I heard from a man who came from Ulan Bator specially for research about Almases that the dead body in question had a great scientific value - told Mr. Choijoa.

Last year he had searched the place of the dead Almas and found only a skull. Sun and wind, snow and rain, and carnivorous beasts and birds had destroyed the corpse of the Almas during that ten years.

Mr. Damdin, who visited the place with Mr. Chimeddorje and Choijoa succeeded in finding several greyish hairs from the head of the Almas.

Mr. Chimmeddorje, manager of the Fruit-growing Station, photographed the skull of the Almas at its place of death. If only he had visited the area and photographed the Almas's corpse ten years ago!

Mr. Damdin has at his disposal the accounts of eye witnesses who met Almases in 1960, 1961, 1962, and August 1963.

One of these eye witnesses, Mr. Batudorje, former army officer and now the brigade leader of the cattle breeders' cooperative in Altantsogutse somon of Bayan-Ölgii province met, at the end of September, in the mountains of Khuren tolgoi (Brawnhill) near the mountain lake Nogonnuur (Green Lake) [49° 37' N, 90°15' E] a strange hairy biped, and twice observed it unobtrusively with field glasses, hiding himself among the rocks at a distance of about 80 - 100 metres.

Mr. Baturdorje met an Almas near the place where, many years before, his father had also met Altain sabdak [?].

Mr. Damdin also talked to a 64 year old Kazakh woman, Khumsai, a member of the peasants' cooperative "Red Dawn" in Tolbo somon Bayan-Ölgii province [48° 24' N, 90°17' E] who had met an Almas at midday on the third of August 1963.

Khumsai and her husband were camping in the desert near Mount Bortu saridak. (It is near the place mentioned in my article, Almas - Mongolian relative of the Snowman [in Russian] in "Contemporary Mongolia", 1958, no. 5, pp. 34-38.) The old woman was ascending a cleft to look after the goats and suddenly heard the flock to shy. Leant of cleaft [?] she saw at a distance of about thirty metres a naked hairy man, very robust and strange, who looked at her unperturbed.

I hope in my following article to give the results of our more better equipped third trip to the Land of Almases.

Editor's Note:The results of this third trip will be so [much] more interesting, as there is no proof that the skull found by Mr. Choija [sic] is that of the Almas seen by him ten years before. The photograph taken by Mr Chimeddorje, kindly sent to this Journal by Prof. Rinčen, show that the skull is of a modern Mongol type, probably of a young woman.

. . . .

Well, that was the situation as of 1964 ie 56 years ago at the time of writing.. The results of the third expedition are not recorded in that journal. Nevertheless, Mr. Damdin did make a total of four expeditions: in 1962, 1963, 1964, and 1965. Therefore, I consider it a good idea to direct you to some other papers for more updated information. All of them can be accessed online after a web search.

- Firstly, we have a paper by archivist Michael Heaney, entitled, "The Mongolian almas: a historical reevaluation of the sighting by Baradiin", *Cryptozoology* vol. 2 (1983), pp 40-52.

In it, he effectively establishes that the alleged sighting by Badzar Baradiin in 1906 was a work of fiction.

- More importantly, we have this article by Prof. Michael Swords, with photographs, about Prof. Rinchen, along with partial translations of his papers of 1958 (in *Contemporary Mongolia*) and 1959. It can be found at: http://thebiggeststudy.blogspot.com/2014/03/rinchen-y-byambyn-and-central-asian.html

- Even more important is that Mr. Damdin produced a manuscript of his four expeditions, containing 312 typewritten pages with 124 photos and 7 figures. Alas! It was sent west to the scientists on the Russian "snowman" project, and appears to have been lost - except for the first four chapters summarising his expeditions. A short English summary has been provided by Michael Trachtengerts at http://alamas.ru/eng/news/Damdin_rev_e. htm. He also provided a link to the surviving four chapters, amounting to 19 pages. Since it is in Russian, which I do not know, I have not translated it. However, Google Translator renders it into quite passable, if rather stilted English. It will be well worth your while to read it, for it details a large number of encounters, some of them in the same year as the expedition. From the evidence provided, it will be hard to resist the conclusion that genuine bipedal primates were really present as late as the mid-1960s.

-      Nevertheless, that was more than 50 years ago, and although the memory of that period remains vivid in the minds of many of us, a lot can happen in half a century. Therefore, your attention is drawn to the following paper:

Ingvar Svanberg and Sabina Ståhlnerg (2017), "Wildmen in Central Asia", *Anthropos* 112(1): 51-61.

The two authors examine the traditions of the area, and note how they have changed over time. They explain that the term, "almas" was originally a generic term for demons, witches, and savages. They believe that it has been the interest shown by foreign cryptozoologists that has consolidated the modern image of the almas as a non-supernatural animal. By the 1990s almas stories consistently treated it as an inhabitant of inaccessible regions, and often refer to abduction and mating with human beings. Invariably they place the events at some indefinite time in the more-or-less distant past, happening to someone else, usually unnamed. In other words, they are urban legends.

     With all due respect, however, it is possible to place another slant on the evidence. Large, uncommon wild animals often have supernatural qualities attributed to them in popular superstitions. It is probably true that cryptozoology has consolidated the view of the almas as a man-like animal, but the only cryptozoologist in the country until the 1960s was Prof. Rinchen himself. He had been studying the matter since 1927, and apparently never regarded it as a subject of superstition. Not only that, but he noted that its range had been shrinking during that period. Furthermore, none of the witnesses who spoke to Damdin provided any supernatural elements.

     Nevertheless, the comment the authors make on the absence of physical evidence is pertinent:

> It is important to stress the lack of furs and hides, because Mongols, Kazak, and other hunters in Central Asia were experts not only in the hunting of any kind of animal but also in conserving hides and animal parts. The interest among rich city dwellers in Saint Petersburg, Moscow, and Beijing toward exotic hides would be enough to encourage any hunter to catch an almas and sell its fur. Siberian and Central Asian fur trade is famous since at least a thousand years, and furs and hides were collected as tax from several peoples in the Russian empire from the 1550s until

our days. Fur markets lined the Russian, Siberian, and northern Chinese borders for centuries. [page 4]

Equally important, the authors claimed that, by the 1990s, no first hand account of a sighting had been recorded for years. As mentioned before, all stories are second hand tales of unnamed persons in an unspecified location an indefinite period in the past. In the paper by Heaney referred to above, mention is made of an alleged encounter in 1974, but nothing else appears to have occurred since them. As the last redoubt of the species was just a 1,000 km^2 patch in the 1960s, it looks like the curtain had finally come down on the almas of Mongolia. Don't you just hate it when that sort of thing happens?

Or has it? I don't suppose the folklorists spoke to anyone near the 1,000km^2 redoubt in the 1990s. Also, on 26 June 2001, an English language newspaper, *The Mongolian Messenger* carried the following story:

A mysterious 'yeti' like creature attacked a driving schoolteacher in the mountains of Gobi-Altai Aimag earlier this month. Ts. Tuvshinjargal was attacked at 12:20 on June 8 in the mountains of Eej Hairhan, Tsogt Soum, by a creature she described as "strong and hairy" which jumped about on its hind legs like a monkey. The creature was frightened off by the loud noise made by Tuvshinjargal's travelling companions and disappeared into the mountains, reported Zuuny Medee. The aimag governor was informed of the attack.

Mount Eej Hairhan, or Khairkhan, is located at approximately 45° N. 90° E, or a couple of hundred miles east of the refuge Damdin explored, and from the Landsat image it looks pretty desolate. On the other hand, the term, "almas" was not cited in the paragraph, and the lady involved appears to have been a person commanding some respect. So, you never know.

Chapter 4

What Are They?

At this point, I feel the need to say a few words about the nature of the animals we are dealing with, because they exist under a variety of names, and because there exist certain ingrained opinions which I consider erroneous.

Firstly, even ignoring the ABSMs of southeast Asia, and concentrating on those in and north of the great mountain ranges, we appear to be dealing with more than one species. Although, the Russians call all of those in their former empire, "snowmen", my impression from reading *In the Footsteps of the Russian Snowman* by the late Dmitri Bayanov is that those inhabiting the vast boreal forests of the north of the continent are similar to the North American bigfoot, while those in the Caucasus, Himalayas, and possibly Central Asia represent a different species, of collection of related species.

The bigfoot or sasquatch is typically described as resembling a gorilla on stilts. In other words, it is like a gorilla would be if it were bipedal, and walked on hind legs in the same proportion to its trunk as a human being's ie six to eight feet [1.8 to 2.4 metres] high and, most importantly, *massive*. Its chest and shoulders are far wider than those of a man of the same height.

Ever since Heuvelmans raised the issue of *Gigantopithecus* in relation to the Himalayan abominable snowman, people have been citing it as the most likely identity of the North American bigfoot - but I have my doubts. *Gigantopithecus* was a huge relative of the orangutan which lived in southern China until about 300,000 years ago. However, its sole remains consist of teeth, and the occasional lower jaw. That makes determining what the rest of its body looked like rather difficult. Its height has been variously estimated as between nine and twelve feet [2.7 to 3.6 metres] - if it were bipedal. We do not know that it was.

It also seems likely that *Gigantopithecus* was sexually dimorphic with regard to size ie the males were much larger than the females. It is true that some minority reports from North America do correlate with the huge stature of a putative male *Gigantopithecus*. The trouble is, this sort of sexual dimorphism is normally associated with harems - for the obvious reason that males have to be outsized in order to protect their females from other males. However, it is pretty certain that the bigfoot/sasquatch is a solitary species.

Moreover, *Gigantopithecus* was an inhabitant of the temperate broad-leafed forests, on which it depended for its diet of coarse, fibrous material and fruit. It is not clear how it could have colonised the northern coniferous forests, and migrated through them to North America, after it had been rendered extinct in its original habitat.

No, much as I would like to believe it, I do not think *Gigantopithecus* is a likely identification for the mystery apes of Siberia and North America.

But when we turn to the yeti, barmanu, almasty, and possibly the almas, it should be obvious that we are dealing with something much slimmer, with proportions more like those of a chimpanzee or a human being. They appear to belong to a different species - or, more likely, a different set of related species. Outwardly similar animals which are nevertheless geographically separate over a wide area have typically separated into different species. Thus, we always used to assume that the orangutans of Borneo and Sumatra belonged to the same species, but in 1996 genetic tests revealed that they were two different species. Then, as recently as 2017, a very small Sumatran population was discovered to be a third species.

With this in mind, let us examine the original "abominable snowman": the yeti of the Himalayas. But, as pointed out at the start of Chapter 1, the area comprises many different languages, and the same animal may be called by different names even in the same language. However, what most westerners do not know is that expeditions in the 1950s heard legends of three different types of "abominable snowman", equivalent to the three gradations of the Three Bears: a very big one called *dzu-teh*, a middle-sized one labelled *yeh-teh* or *meh-teh*, and a mysterious small one, the *teh-lma*. Reinhold Messner showed that the *chemo* can be identified with the Himalayan brown bear, so the *dzu-teh* is the same thing, while the *teh-lma* may be some sort of gibbon. But what about the middle-sized one, the yeti? As a result of Magraner's work, it is pretty hard to deny that it really is an unknown species of ape.

A species' behaviour repertoire and its social system are just as much part of its genetic make-up as its physical features. Among advanced, more intelligent species, it can be varied to a great extent, but not indefinitely. As useful analogy is that of a rubber template; it can be stretched, but still retains the relationship between the parts, and always tends to revert to its default setting. (The same is true, of course, of human beings. All humans societies, no matter how apparently dissimilar, are variations on a theme.)

With respect to their daily cycle of activity, Magraner recorded more or less equal numbers of barmanu sightings by day and by night. However, considering the fact that potential human witnesses are far less active at night, this would imply that the barmanu is more active at night. Similarly, the Caucasus creatures were typically sighted during the day, when the witnesses were active, Koffmann suggested their eyes possess a tapetum evolved for night vision.

All this is strongly in contrast to the other higher monkeys and apes. It would be rare to discover a chimpanzee, gorilla, or baboon active once the sun set.

Whereas orangutans are solitary animals, chimpanzees, bonobos, gorillas, and even the higher monkeys, live in small to medium sized groups. However, the barmanu and almasty appear to be essentially solitary, although almasties may come together temporarily in small groups.

All this confirms what I said in the introduction: the ABSMs of the world have remained unknown to science because they are basically solitary and nocturnal.

As far as height goes, the barmanu is similar to that of the local human inhabitants, the almasty of the Caucasus somewhat taller, although not as tall or as broad as the North American bigfoot.

A useful matter to consider is their epigamic features ie traits which have evolved primarily as social signals. Thus, among human beings, there are good practical reasons why a man should have broad shoulders and a woman broad hips, but the only reason a man has a beard is to display to the world that he is a man - and not a boy or a woman.

In our own species the common epigamic features are long hair on the head, and everted lips. (Monkeys and apes all possess thin lips.) With men it is the beard and, in some cases, hair on the chest. With women it is protruding breasts, demonstrating that she is no longer a girl, but is capable of feeding a baby. (Female apes are flat chested when not lactating.)

With this in mind, we note that both the barmanu and the almasty possess long hair on the head, the latter more than the former. Along with bipedalism, does this indicate that they are closely related to our own species? Maybe, but if so, they have diverged sharply from the main trunk of the family tree in their solitary, largely nocturnal lifestyle.

Male almasties have no beards. On the other hand, the barmanu possesses a "hairy goitre or sort of beard", though it is not depicted on the drawings. Probably it is not a genuine beard, dependent on the chin, but a general hairiness about the throat area. With respect to the females, there are multiple reports of long breasts, but there is no way of knowing whether or not they were lactating. In many cases, neither breasts nor penis were recorded. Were these really non-lactating females, or were they males whose genitals were simply overlooked? Most of these did possess a "hairy goitre or sort of beard", which therefore may not be limited to males. (Nevertheless, we must remember the female almasty who spent a whole week living in a vegetable patch. Although her breasts were elongated, she obviously did not have a baby to go back to.)

All told, it appears that the only epigamic feature they share with humanity is the length of the head hair.

As I explained in the introduction to Part I, it appears to be an article of belief among French and Russian cryptozoologists that the "hominids" of the former Soviet Union and the Himalayas are "relict Neanderthals". This is certainly false. The Neanderthals were human - a different species of humanity, to be sure, but nevertheless human, a sister species which diverged from ours approximately 800,000 years ago.

Firstly, it is questionable that they were covered with a full pelage of body hair, like an ape. I know that one anthropologist believes they were, on the basis that they lived during the Ice Age, but did not wear sewn clothing, only blankets and ponchos. Nevertheless, it has been shown that human ancestors lost the majority of their body hair - became "naked apes" - in Africa about 1.2 million years ago. We know this by examination of the genes for melanin, which reveal that we developed black skin about that time. This was long before the our lineage separated from that of the Neanderthals. Perhaps the Neanderthals were more hairy than us but, if so, they are unlikely to have been as hairy as an ape. Moreover, it is likely that possessed typical human epigamic features, such as beards and everted lips.

In any case, their brains were, if anything, slightly larger than ours. Whether this equated to a similar IQ is a moot point, but it was certainly a human intelligence. They possessed a major gene for speech. They had a sophisticated stone tool culture; they hunted big game, they used fire, and they buried their dead.

Not only did they live in groups, but it is pretty certain that they possessed the fundamental human social system of marriage, for the same reason our ancestors evolved it: because their large brained offspring, with their lengthy childhood, required the care of both mother and father. Again, remember the female almasty who *lived* settled for a week in a vegetable patch (p 55). Can you imagine any behaviour less human than that? A *sapiens* or Neanderthal woman would have returned every night to her husband or parents. In fact, it is unlikely she would have been alone in the first place. She would have arrived with at least two or three other women.

No, we may rest assured that the "hominids" of the Caucasus and Himalayas are not the last, degenerative remnant of *Homo neanderthalensis*. They are animals.

No discussion of the matter would be complete without a discussion of Zana, whose story was uncovered by Russian researchers in the 1960s. She was a female almasty captured in Abkhazia, where such creatures are known as *abnauayu*, and died sometime in the 1880s or 1890s. According to oral tradition, she was delivered over to a local nobleman, chained and shackled, and lodged in a strong enclosure. With black skin, and covered with reddish black hair, she was tall, massive, and immensely strong, with teeth which could crack walnuts, and a broad face with like jaws like a muzzle.

But her expression was purely animal and, despite becoming more or less tame over the years, she never learned to speak. She also preferred to go naked, even in cold weather, and could not endure warm rooms. No matter what the weather, she always slept in a hole she had dug in the ground.

The remarkable thing was that she bore several children to the local men, who were apparently far from fussy in their sexual escapades. The two sons and two daughters who survived were described as dark skinned and powerfully built, but with hardly any of their mother's facial anatomy. Surprisingly, these children possessed human reason, and were able to talk.

The researchers were unable to locate Zana's grave, but they did unearth the bones of her son, Khwit. In the opinion of a couple of Moscow Anthropologists, it displayed a combination of primitive and modern features. As such, it attracted the attention of Prof. Grover Krantz, an American physical anthropologist with both knowledge of the Neanderthals, and a lifetime fascination with the sasquatch. Having examined it, he declared it was essentially a normal human skull.

Now, if an almasty/abnauayu is capable of interbreeding with *Homo sapiens*, the two species must be very closely related. Nevertheless, we have a quandary. The mother was essentially an animal, her hybrid offspring essentially human. Something is wrong here. The story has become distorted, and the most likely source of the distortion would be at the earliest link ie Zana herself.

At least, that was my original assessment, and in 2013 it was confirmed in a startling manner. A professor of human genetics, Dr. Bryan Sykes examined samples of DNA for one of Khwit's teeth, and from known grandchildren of Zana. The results were clear: Zana had been an African. What had she been doing in Abkhazia? One suggestion was that she had been brought to the Caucasus as part of the Ottoman slave trade, and that when the Russians occupied the area and abolished slavery, she was left behind, possibly having gone feral.

But what about her unusual physical characteristics, and her full covering of body hair? I suspect that, because the locals had never seen an African before, they assumed she must have been an abnauaya. After that, oral tradition assimilated her features to the traditional description of the abnauaya. She was probably never hairy after all. But that still doesn't explain why she never learned to speak even a word of the local language. Perhaps she was autistic, or otherwise mentally retarded, and had been abandoned to become a "wild child" because of that. We'll never know.

Poor Zana! Her life must have been wretched. But she had nothing to do with the creatures of the Caucasus.

PART II

EUROPE

Of course, I hear you say, Europe is the one place where you would never find any mystery primates. Yes, technically, the Caucasus is part of Europe, and European Russia also contains vast tracts of forest where they could hide. But what we think of as Europe: the western and central part of the continent, the homeland of Western civilisation - that is too heavily populated and seeped in so much history, it is impossible to imagine any ABSM lurking in what is left of its wilderness.

But is it possible that such thing existed in the past? Bigfoots which have been "forgotten", as the title of this book implies? Some would point to the classical fauns, satyrs, and sileni: beings human above the waist, but a goat or horse below. However, I don't think so.

These myths are better explained as the products of magico-religious rituals. In order to maintain the fertility of their flocks and herds, prehistoric pastoralists would perform dances dressed as their livestock. Eventually, they came to believe they were impersonating nature spirits: minor, anonymous gods under the headship of Pan, the great god with a goat's lower regions.The fertility aspects of the rituals, and the fact that they were performed by the herdsmen themselves, is the reason these beings are always perceived as male, and lustful.

As a boy, I was fascinated by the Greek myths, and developed an almost encyclopaedic knowledge of them, but I am unaware of any myth concerning actual "wild men". Nevertheless, the image of the wild man was a common motif throughout medieval Europe, appearing on coats of arms, decorations on buildings, tapestries, and even the popular miracle plays. Almost invariably he was depicted as naked and covered with hair, often wielding a knobbly club. The common English term was *woodwose*, or simply *wose*, which possibly means "wood being", the second element being related to the word, "was". Readers of Tolkien's *The Lord of the Rings* will remember the woses.

Of course, this does not mean that such beings ever actually existed, any more than did that other decorative figure on buildings, the half-vegetable Green Man. The wild man is essentially a man who lives like a beast. He need be no more than a figment of our imagination, a potent reminder that the barrier which separates us from the animal world is thin and fragile.

Just the same, there is always the possibility that once bipedal primates similar to those of the Caucasus existed in the heartland of Europe, and have gradually disappeared with the advance of civilisation. In fact, there is one corner of the continent where, if you are to believe the legends, the wild man hung out until quite recently, if not even to the present day, and that is the Pyrenees, the mountain range separating Spain from France.

At this point, I should explain that the chapters in this section are translations from the French from a small journal of restricted distribution named *Bipedia*[21], edited and published by a certain M. François de Sarre. His overall purpose was to propound a crackpot theory of "initial bipedalism" that all four legged vertebrates are descended from a bipedal ancestor. Nevertheless, the journal also attracted authors interested in the sort of mystery primates with which we are concerned. So here goes . . .

---

[21] Available online at
http://initial.bipedalism.pagesperso-orange.fr/bipedia.htm.

Chapter 5

The Wild Man of the Pyrenees

"L'homme sauvage dans les Pyrénées et la survivance des néanderthaliens," (The wild man of the Pyrenees and the survival of the Neanderthals)
by Michel Raynal, *Bipedia* 3 (1989):1-16

On 6 June 1972, before the Archaeological Commission of Narbonne, an unexpected paper on "The abominable snowman in the Pyrenees" was read out by a teacher of French from that town, Paul Ornières (Ornières, 1972). Having heard about the matter in 1981, I immediately contacted the widow Ornières, who kindly put at my disposal her husband's library, and in particular, his as yet unpublished study on "The Neanderthals in the Pyrenees", written two years later (Ornières, 1974).

[For the sake of brevity, I shall pass over a dissertation of more than two pages concerning Neanderthal man, and the nature of various unknown bipedal apes in the Caucasus, the (then) USSR, and Indo-China.]

THE THEME OF THE BEAR KIDNAPPER

Throughout the whole of the Pyrenees there runs the legend of John-of-the-Bear, the most popular tale in this region: it exists in dozens of versions, constructed around the following central core: a bear kidnaps a young girl, carries her into his cave, and holds her prisoner there by closing the grotto with a heavy slab. He begets a son, hairy and strong like a bear, as per his name, who, on growing up, becomes strong enough to move the slab aside and escape; he becomes a blacksmith and, after a number of adventures, which notably evoke the Cycle of the Round Table, which were obviously added subsequently, as can be established by comparison with the Basque legends of *Basa Jaun* (see below). A human-bear hybridisation is, of course, genetically impossible, but does it really relate back to a bear? The manual dexterity lent to the offspring of these unnatural loves suggests a primate hand, not the paw of a bear (as well as the episode of the slab, as far as the father is concerned).

Might it relate back to a confused memory of a hybridisation between a type of primitive human and a women? But to continue ...[22]

We return to this theme of a bear kidnapping a young woman in the "bear's festival", as at Prats-de-Mollo, Arles-sur-Tech, or Saint-Laurent-de-Cerdans in the eastern Pyrenees. The bear's festival also exists at Ariège, and Daniel Vigne was inspired by this for a sequence in his film *Le Retour de Martin Guerre* ["The Return of Martin Guerre"]. In all these cases, a person playing the "bear", often armed with a stick or a club, carries off a girl, and is pursued by the hunters, who end by capturing him, killing him (or shaving, or castrating him), and liberating the young woman. Indeed, it follows very precisely the theme of the "wild man hunts" in the medieval carnivals and music festivals of central Europe (Bernheimer 1952).

THE PYRENEAN TRADITION

Numerous Pyrenean traditions are still alive regarding the Wild Men. At Arles-sur-Tech, *simiots*, "frightful monsters, with split teeth and crooked hands, roam the night on the rooftops, descending into the houses down the chimney, uttering mournful howls (Blanc 1979); tradition holds that it was the local saints, Abdon and Sennen who conquered them. Furthermore, the so-called "bear" of the above mentioned carnival of Arles-sur-Tech carnival is always called the *simiot*[23].

In Haute-Ariège, the Wild Man was called the *ome pelut* ("hairy man") or *iretgge*, which might have been a corruption of "heretic".

> At an undetermined period, towards the XII or XIII
> centuries, there lived in the forest of Barthes, two wild men
> (*iretgges*), naked, hairy, each armed with a knotty stick,
> coming from no-one knows where, having as shelter only the
> caves of our mountains and, as sole nourishment, only the
> spontaneous products of the soil or whatever game they could
> capture.

In order to get rid of these undesirables, one villager had the idea of leaving some red shorts in the forest where the *iretgges* used to frequent,

---

[22] Note: in this, and other quotes, the spaces indicated by three dots were present in the original.
[23] The word obviously derives from the Latin *simia*, a monkey or ape.

so as to attract their attention. The villagers sprang onto them, and made them prisoners, as they were hindered in their movements (Piniès 1978).

In this legend one in fact meets the old myth of the Wild Man was his club, but also, and this is even more significant, the old legend about a method of capturing monkeys[24], by making them put on boots, which renders their gait clumsy, which one finds in Africa (Heuvelmans 1980). The question which is posed is to know which local "ape" would have been able to inspire this legend, which is also recounted in the Aude with clogs in place of shorts or boots (Maffre 1939).

From another case, where someone lends an *iretgge* a scimitar, it is evident that the memory of the former presence of Moors in the Midi has been superimposed. The presumed lewdness of the wild men, their nocturnal habits (the night being favourable to demons in the popular imagination) can only accentuate their diabolic character, thus heretical in the eyes of the good people . . . The characters in which they approach the billy goat (see later), thus in the popular image of the Devil, must have also contributed.

BASA-JAUN, THE WILD LORD OF THE BASQUE COUNTRY

In the Basque country, both French and Spanish, there run legends of the *Basa-Jaun*, the local Wild Man (or more exactly, the Wild Lord):

> *Basa-Jaun* does not differ significantly from a wild beast.
> He is covered with hair like a bear; he feeds only on herbs or
> game; he does not leave the mountains or the forests; he is
> cruel, he is a thief. [...] He is not subject to infirmities; he
> always retains a strength without equal; he is insensitive to the
> inclemency of the seasons; he walks around by day and
> night . . . (Cerquand 1875-1882)

The one surnamed "billy goat man" is accused of haunting the shepherds' cabins in the mountains, where he comes to warm himself next to the fire, or to simply purloin their milk and their cheese, such a veritable parasite (Webster 1879). Of course, in various tales, he is accused of carrying off women and begetting on them young which are hairy and uncommonly strong (Sébillot 1904-1907), which reminds us of the legend of John-of-the-Bear. We may add that he seems to possess a

---

[24] or apes, the words are identical in French

long head of hair (including *Basa-Andere*, his wife), and that many of his exploits take place at night.

Of course, this character is present in numerous Basque tales, and is considered (or was recently considered) as a real animal; that Goupil [the fox] of the *Romance of Renart*, as well as the other animals of the forest, speak like men, does not mean that the fox, the *Vulpes vulpes* of the zoologists, does not exist! Quite the contrary, a zoological (and in particular ethological) reading of this medieval masterpiece tells us a lot about this animal; that it lives in a den, that it is omnivorous, but mainly carnivorous, that is it cunning to the extent of playing dead, etc, etc., and on the anatomical plan it must resemble its "cousin" Ysengrin the wolf (*Canis lupus*), but with a red pelt - all things perfectly exact, and amply demonstrated thereafter.

Thus, therefore, two centuries ago at most, the woodcutters of the Iraty Forest used to affirm having encountered its footprints, and others to have heard it, and the memory was still being recently perpetuated in the evenings around the fire:

> "Two mountaineers, so it has been well heard, at night, among the rocks, when they were desperately searching for some stray beasts [. . .]

Lost in the mist, they were ascertaining their position by identifying themselves with the piercing cry which they call the *irrintzina*, when one of the two realised that it was the *Basa-Jaun* who was imitating him! (Duny-Pétré 1960).

If a number of the stories are extremely mythified, in fact truly fabulous tales, there are some which are astonishingly realistic; I wish to tender as proof only the one about the "*Basa Jaun* at the *cayolar*", which deserves to be cited in full:

> There were once two shepherds in a shepherd's hut. One evening, after supper, they were watching some chestnuts grilling in the fire. While they were roasting, they lay down a moment, for they had become very tired, during the day, guarding their flock, and sleep overtook them.
>
> A noise coming from the door wakes them up; they await something which is agitating the latch of the door. Terror seizes them, for they say among themselves that it is surely

Basa Jauna. They remain silent, not speaking, and pretend to sleep.

They were in no way mistaken: they see a Wild Lord enter, all black and covered with hair. He approaches them, and they feel a rough, trembling hand pass over their faces. They think that it is all over for them, that the Wild Lord is going to devour them, and they are so afraid that they can hardly breathe. But no: *Basa Juana* sets himself down in front of the fire, warms himself, and retrieving the chestnuts from the ashes, eats them all. While eating, he is all the time watching to see if the shepherds are waking up. The latter, scared to death, don't even move at all.

The Wild Lord, after having eaten the chestnuts, gets up, takes whatever he likes in the cabin, and departs without doing harm to anyone."

A tale? Yes, certainly, but one which has an astonishing aroma of authenticity: one would almost believe it a typical report from the Caucasus, such as Marie-Jeanne Koffmann has collected.

HISTORIC TESTIMONIES

In the Pyrenean Wild Man dossier, there is not only folklore: we also possess *testimonies* concerning the hairy humanoid creatures observed right up to a recent period, and this precisely in the country of the *Basa Jaun*.

It is thus that a naval engineer, Julien David Leroy, in his work on forest exploitation in the Pyrenees (1776), makes mention of several stories of feral children, like the celebrate Victor of l'Aveyron, to whom the late lamented François Truffaut consecrated one of his most beautiful films (*L'Enfant Sauvage* [The Wild Child]): these are only children abandoned, and therefore returned to the wild state, unrelated to our subject. In revenge, he cites a much more troubling case.

Two years ago [therefore in 1774] the herdsmen of the Yraty Forest, near Saint-Jean-de-Pied-de-Port, often noticed an wild man who inhabited the rocks of this forest. This man was of great height, hairy as a bear, and alert as a chamois, of cheerful disposition, with the appearance of a gentle character, since he did harm to nothing. He often used to visit the cabins without carrying off anything; he knew neither bread, milk, or cheese; his great pleasure was to make the flocks run, and to disperse them by making great peels of laughter, but he never did them any harm. The herdsmen used to often set their dogs after him; then he would run off like a dart, and never let them approach very close. One single time, he came in the morning to the door of the cabin of workmen who were making oars, and which had retained a great abundance of snow fallen during the night; he stood erect at the door which he was holding with two hands, and was laughing as he looked at the workmen. One of these people softly slid [forward] so as to attempt to seize him by his leg; as soon as he saw him approach, he redoubled his laugh; then he escaped. It was judged that this man would have been thirty years old; as this forest is of great extent, and communicates with immense woods belonging to Spain, it is presumed that this might be some young child who was lost, and who had found the means to subsist on the vegetation.

This last explanation shows a great naivety, inspired by the legend of the hairy hermit, who wishes to live in the wild and ends up acquiring a hairy pelage, a legend bereft, it must be said, of all foundation.

Other testimonies have been collected by Gomez-Tabanera (1978); last century [written 1989] a "mujer salvaje" (wild woman) was pointed out in the mountains of Cantabria. Nicknamed "la Osa de Andara" (the she-bear of Andara), she used to take refuge in the grottoes; "her arms and legs were hairy, with a pelage comparable to that of a bear". She used to feed on milk, chestnuts, roots, raw maize, fruit and berries (strawberries, gooseberries, etc), honeycomb, but also occasionally little goats.

"I have seen her devour one of these animals", writes Joaquin Fusté y Garcés in 1875: "at that moment she would by roaring like a real savage beast and flashing lightning with her eyes."

She used to possess a sort of tray or pan for the milk, and a knife fashioned out of a piece of horn, and she wore around her lions "a sort of skirt of which one could not tell whether it was made of hair or cloth."

Sculpture of the so-called "She-bear of Cornellana" (Asturias, Spain).
Photo: J. M. Gomez-Tabanera

Gomez-Tabanera also reports the legend of the foundation of the monastery of San Salvador de Cornellana in Asturia. A child had formerly been carried off by a monster termed an *osa* (she-bear). After a long search, they were both discovered in the forest, "the above-mentioned she-bear suckling the child, which was quietly resting in her hirsute pelage." The lord of Doriga , in order to thank heaven for the miracle, had the monastery constructed and the scene sculptured (see photo)[25].

There is perhaps a still more recent testimony, reported by Daniel Fabre (1969), in his study on John-of-the-Bear:

> Mme Gomez (born 1926), an inhabitant of Lézignan (Aude), recounted to us how, in the village of her birth, Cuevas-Bajas (Málaga Province) around about 1920, a young couple (the Palmares) departed into the Sierra Morena in order to tend cattle. They used to live isolated in a cabin. One day, when her husband was absent, the young woman disappeared. The villagers did not pursue their search very long, thinking that she had been devoured by the wild beasts which infested the region. But some time later the woman returned to her home and related her astonishing story.

---

[25] Although this is "just" a legend, I don't find it extraordinary. Female animals which have just lost their young have been known to adopt babies of completely different species.

She had been carried off by an ape when she was washing her linen in the river. It had led her into his grotto and had raped her. During its absence, she had succeeded in running away. Some months later, she gave birth to a daughter who was baptized Anica, and who was better known as "the daughter of the orang-outang" (*la hija del orang-outang*) [N.B.: more exactly, orang-utan]. She had partially inherited the physique of her father's: long arms, hairy body; her face was that of an ape in the lower part, that of her mother in the upper part. Furthermore, this daughter afterwards had two sons who are still alive in the town of Labisbal (Gerona Province): the first is absolutely normal, but the other is nicknamed "the cheese" because of his simian ugliness.

Man x ape hybridisation is generally held to be impossible, although the possibility has not been genuinely explored for ethical reasons. However, the case of the childbirth at Vichy (a girl who used to live held captive by her father in a caravan, in the company of a chimpanzee, and who gave birth to a monstrous stillborn baby) is well documented, and none the less disturbing (Duvic 1973). Nevertheless, such a hybrid, if it existed, would be non-viable: the anatomical differences between man and the Pongidae (anthropoid apes) is such that it is hard to see, to give one example, an intermediate state between a running foot on the one hand, and a tree-climbing prehensile one (transformed into a hand) on the other . . . In the case of Mme Palmares, with the usual reservations (second hand testimony, prior to the birth of the informant), the hybrid in question is hairy, her upper limbs are long, and "the bottom part of her face" is simian: that would mean a receding chin, and perhaps no visible lips . . . That the father was designated an orang-utan should not be taken seriously: it is obviously a general term; today we talk of an "ape-man" or a King Kong. Besides, its cave-dwelling habits have nothing to do with the arboreal ones of the big red ape of Sumatra and Borneo .

[The author then continues with a discussion of the identity of the Wild Man of the Pyrenees almost as long as the rest of the article, attempting to relate it to the *almasties* of the Caucasus, and to Neanderthal Man.]

BERNHEIMER, Richard, 1952 *Wild Men in the Middle Ages*. Cambridge, Harvard University Press

BLANC, Dominique, 1979 *Récits et Contes Populaires de Catalogne* [Reports and popular tales of Catalonia], Paris, Gallimard, vol. 1: 133-138, 146

CERQUAND, J. F., 1875-1882 *Légendes et Récits Populaires du Pays Basque*. [Popular legends and reports of the Basque country] Paris, Ribaud: 10, 70

DUNY-PETRE, Pierre, 1960 *Basa Jauna*, le Seigneur Sauvage, dans les Légendes Basques [*Basa-Jaun*, the Wild Lord, in Basque legends], *Bulletin de la Société des Sciences, Lettres et Arts de Bayonne*, no 92-94, 87-105, 120-159, 177-222

DUVIC, Patrice, 1973*Monstres et Monstruosités* [Monsters and monstrosities], Paris, Albin Michel: 9- 29 [26]

FABRE, Daniel, 1968-1969 Recherches sur Jean-de-l'Ours, Conte Populaire. [Research on John-of-the-Bear, a popular tale], *Folklore*, Carcassonne, Vol. 21(3-4): 2-41 and Vol. 22(2): 2-36

GOMEZ-TABAERA, Jose-Manuel, 1978 La Conseja del Hombre Salvaje en la Tradición Popular de la Peninsula Iberica [The myth of the wild man in the popular tradition of the Iberian Peninsula] in *Homenaje a Julio Caro Baroja*, Madrid: Centro do Investigaciones Sociologicas: 471-509

HEUVELMANS, Bernard, 1980 *Les Bêtes Humaines d'Afrique* [The human beasts of Africa], Paris, Plon

LEROY, Julien David, 1776 *Mémoire sur les Travaux qui ont Rapport à l'Exploitation de la Nature dans les Pyrénées* [Memoire on the works in relation to the exploitation of nature in the Pyrenees], London: 8-9

MAFFRE, J., 1939 L'Homme Sauvage et le Lait [The wild man and milk], *Folklore*, Carcassonne, no. 12: 31-34

ORNIERES, Paul, 1972 (Communication). *Bulletin de la Commission Archéologique de Narbonee*, vol. 34: 36

---

[26] A more detailed discussion of this case can be found at http://www.macroevolution.net/anencephale-de-vichy.html (accessed 2.7.20)

ORNIERES, Paul,1974 Les Néanderthaliens dans les Pyrénées. [The Neanderthals in the Pyrenees], unpublished study, Narbonne, October: 1-9

PINIES, Jean-Pierre, 1978 *Récits et Contes Populaires de Catalogne* [Reports and popular tales of Catalonia], Paris, Gallimard, vol. 1: 110-119

SEBILLOT, Paul, 1904-1907 *Le Folklore de France*, Paris, E. Guilmoto.

WEBSTER, Wentworth, 1879 *Basque Legends.* London, Griffith and Farran: 47 - 63

. . . .

Now, lest you imagine that this is all something of the past, I shall finish with this story which I took from the excellent *Bigfoot Encounters*[27] website.

In June 1993 a group of speleologists (scientific study and exploration of caves) prepared to spend the night at the ruins of a church near Collada de Vallgrasa in the Catalan Pyrenees Mountain Range of Spain. They heard strange noises resembling those of an enraged cat. When they came close to the church's large doorway, the scientists saw a frightened, weird, shaggy creature, approximately 1.5 meters (5 feet tall) flee from the building. He was of enormous bulk. The *wild man* appeared again in the woods between Farga de Bebié and Ripoll (Gerona). Two *hairy beings* pounced on two paleontologists then ran away from them.
(Citation: De la Rubio Muñoz and Dr. Myra Shackley, *Wildmen: Yeti, Sasquatch and the Neanderthal Enigma* (London: Thames & Hudson, 1983) ISBN 0-500-01298-9 (also published as *Still Living?: Yeti, Sasquatch and the Neanderthal Enigma* ISBN 0-500-01298-9)

Yes, I know the dates are discordant. I haven't read the original document, but I presume "1993" is a misprint. Incredible as it may seem, the file is not yet closed on the subject, as some recent

____

[27] http://www.bigfootencounters.com/creatures/basajaun.htm

Spanish blogs have indicated[28]. In 1993 a group of shepherds did see a strange creature in a tree just 90 metres from them. In 2008 and 2009, two expeditions entered the area and, although they did not see any "wild man", they did discover broken timber arrayed in manners not usual for human beings, but also recorded in North America and suspected of being made by bigfoot, as well as some indistinct footprints. Finally, in 2011 a humanoid figure was photographed cavorting in an area where no human being would be expected to be, acting in a quite non-human manner.

None of this can be considered hard evidence, but it still makes you wonder.

---

[28] I translated them on one of my own blogs. See
http://malcolmscryptids.blogspot.com/2016/02/the-search-for-wild-man-of-pyrenees.html and
http://malcolmscryptids.blogspot.com/2016/01/a-photo-of-wild-man-of-pyrenees.html

Chapter 6

The Barcelona Satyr

Une figuration de l'homme sauvage dans les Pyrénées?
(A Representation of the Wild Man in the Pyrenees?)
by Michel Raynal, *Bipedia* 4, 1990, pp 16-18

ABSTRACT : *In 1760, an article was published about a so-called "satyr" shown in Barcelona (Spain) : It was a human-like hairy creature with some strange features, such as "ears like a tiger's" or "whiskers like a cat's". An illustration is available, but it was made from the article, not by a first-hand witness ; from an analysis of the text, having in mind the data summarized in Raynal's previous article for (RAYNAL 1989), this creature seems to be a relict Neanderthal from the Pyrenees.*

In an earlier article for *Bipedia* (RAYNAL 1989), I analysed the diverse elements, noting the reports on the Hairy Wild Men, leading one to think that the Neanderthals survived in the Pyrenees, up to the eighteenth century at least.

In this regard, it must be mentioned that the recent survival of the Neanderthals in this region had been envisaged earlier by several Soviet researchers, notably Dmitri Bayanov and Igor Bourtsev, such that they had already wished to interpret the case of the hairy wild man of the Iraty Forest in the Basque country from 1774 in the same way (BAYANOV & BOURTSEV 1976). This unpardonable forgetfulness on my part should be corrected on the earliest occasion .

Dmitri Bayanov, of the Darwin Museum in Moscow, has recently had the kindness to communicate a very interesting document which deserves to be added to the dossier. It is taken from the journal, *Moskovska Vedomosti*, No. 55, of 11 July 1760, and is reproduced in the book, *Dessins Populaires Russes* [Popular Russian Drawings], Saint Petersburg, 1900, p. 139:

"From Spain, a newspaper reports with respect to this drawing (Fig.1) that a foreigner has brought to Barcelona a satyr whose monstrous aspect is attracting numerous spectators. This animal has the head, forehead, eyes and eyebrows of a man, the ears of a tiger, red cheeks, the whiskers of a cat, the beard of a goat, the mouth of a lion in which there is a bony border to the tooth line, and arms which resemble those of a man, but covered down to the hands with hairs of different colours; as well as on the whole of the body. Its height is 5 feet 3 inches (1m 60), and it eats only bread and milk."

Fig. 1: Représentation du *satyre espagnol* de 1760 (tirée du livre *Dessins Populaires Russes*, cf. texte)

The origins of the creature not being given precisely, it could have been captured far from Spain by the said "foreigners"[29] who exhibited it as a fairground curiosity. However, it seems more logical to suppose that it came from the Pyrenees, one of the last places in Europe where the Neanderthals still subsisted until the end of the eighteenth century (HEUVELMANS & PORSHNEV 1974, HEUVELMANS 1986). In that

---

[29] The text mentions only one.

case, the "foreigners" in question would have had some chance of being French!

It is clear in any case that the drawing was not based on an eye witness; it turns out to be a *traditional* representation of the Hairy Wild Man, to which the illustrator has added some features borrowed from the text, which he has naively placed at the foot of the page the reported expressions. That is particularly manifested in the cloven feed, evidently "deduced" from the title of the article; a real, self-respecting "satyr" would have to have the feet of a goat! It has, however, been demonstrated that this is a naive visualisation of the Neanderthal's foot, adapted to the mountain, "to know the goat's foot", as is popularly said (HEUVELMANS & PORSHNEV 1974, HEUVELMANS 1980, RAYNAL 1989).

Coming back to the description, bearing in mind the fact that the expressions must be especially placed at the foot of the page (and materialised in the form of a visual pun, as in the sketches of Raymond Devos), but *interpreted*: one shall refer back to the authoritative study made by Bernard HEUVELMANS (1980) on the "Different peoples of Ancient Ethiopia" (headless men, goat-footed men, elephant-eared men, sucklings of bitches, etc, etc) which the ancients loved to situate in Africa.

First of all, one should not be misled by the classification of the creature as a "satyr". These days, any sensational journalist worthy of the name would label it "the Wild Man of Barcelona" or "King Kong of Catalonia". In the mid-eighteenth century, it was the word, satyr which drew the crowds, the satyr which rapes pretty girls being the prototype of the Hairy Wild Man: even in 1816, Lorenz Oken described the chimpanzee under the generic name of *Pan*, which it still possesses!

By "ears of a tiger", one must obviously understand pointed ears: either the same shape as the peak of a tent, effectively pointed, or with a brush of hair (as in a lynx, for example) producing the same illusion.

The body is covered with hair, but not the face (hence the checks are visible, even said to be red), doubtless with the exception of some very sparse hairs, like those of a cat's whiskers.

The "mouth of a lion" can obviously not be applied to the appearance of the teeth, since the latter were absent (see the following point); evidently, the expression means an enormous mouth, very wide; as for the bony border in the place of teeth, Bernard Heuvelmans (personal communication) judiciously attributes it to the gums of a toothless old man.

All these characteristics have been registered in many *current* testimonies on the Hairy Wild Men of North and Central Asia (notably in the Caucasus and Mongolia), and can be found in the frozen specimen studied by Heuvelmans (see the illustration in the previous *Bipedia*); the extreme hairiness except on the face, with the exception of some downy hairs: "on the cheeks there are some little, short hairs, very sparse, disposed a little like the whiskers of a cat", writes Heuvelmans with respect to the frozen specimen studied by him (HEUVELMANS & PORSHNEV 1974: 219); the widely split mouth, the pointed ears, the human height, etc. One can even wonder if the claimed goat's beard is not a naive description of the vocal sac designed to amplify the cries (as with the siamang gibbon) equally characteristic of the Asiatic wild men.

The feeding is also instructive, as the penchant for milk by the Pyrenian Hairy Wild Men, like the Asiatic ones, has been raised and is an object of tentative explanation (RAYNAL 1989).

Definitively, it does seem that the "satyr" exhibited in Barcelona in 1760 cannot be anything but a typical Hairy Wild Man, i.e. a late Neanderthal, probably originating in the Pyrenees.

REFERENCES

BAYANOV, Dmitri & Igor BOURTSEV, 1976 : *On Neanderthal vs. Paranthropus - Current Anthropology*, vol. 17 (2): 312-316 (June).

HEUVELMANS, Bernard,1980 : *Les Bêtes Humaines d'Afrique* [The Human Beasts of Africa]- Paris, Plon.

HEUVELMANS, Bernard, 1986 :Annotated checklist of apparently unknown animals with which cryptozoology is concerned, *Cryptozoology*, 5 : 1-26.

HEUVELMANS, Bernard & Boris PORCHNEV, 1974 :*L'Homme de Néanderthal est toujours vivant* [Neanderthal Man is still alive] - Paris, Plon.

RAYNAL, Michel 1989 : L'homme sauvage dans les Pyrénées et la survivance des néanderthaliens, *Bipedia* 3: 1-16, C.E.R.B.I., Nice [See previous chapter.]

. . . .

From what you have read so far, you will be aware that I do not share the Franco-Russian doctrine that the "wild men" of Asia are relict Neanderthals. I also have grave doubts about the genuineness of the Minnesota Iceman, which Heuvelmans described. Nevertheless, the author has done a pretty good job of comparing the Barcelona satyr to the known characteristics of the Caucasian almasties. Is there a more mundane explanation?

A Barbary macaque (*Macaca sylvanus*)? It has been known since classical times, and exists even today in Gibraltar. I suspect that, had a Barbary macaque been exhibited in Barcelona in 1760, there would be people in the audience who would recognize it. Just the same, I also suspect that it would have been sufficiently novel to be able to draw the crowds without any "hype". But no matter how much hype the foreigner produced, it would be hard to palm off a quadrupedal monkey no more than 25 inches long with a vestigial tail, as a bipedal satyr 5 ft 3 inches high.

A chimpanzee? It would have to be an adult. There is a good reason why such an animal would be a novelty in 1760. At that period no white person ever ventured into the interior of West Africa. From Ramona and Desmond Morris' book, *Men and Apes* (1966), it appears that only three chimpanzees and one orangutan ever made it to Europe in the whole of the seventeenth and eighteenth centuries. They had to be purchased from the natives, were usually young, and didn't last long. In other words, a fully grown (and dangerous) chimpanzee was not something which would be casually picked up by some passing sailor.

So what was the Barcelona satyr? And what was the original source of the information? Your guess is as good as mine.

PART III

LATIN AMERICA

Of course, we have all heard of the bigfoot or sasquatch of English speaking North America, but it is not well known that similar animals are alleged to exist south of the Rio Grande, and right down into South America.

One of them has even been given with a scientific name: *Ameranthropoides loysi*, Loys' ape, which was allegedly shot, and certainly photographed by a Swiss geologist, François de Loys in 1920. It was supposed to have been a giant, tailless spider monkey, but is now generally recognized as a hoax.

Currently, several investigators are searching for something called a *mapinguary*, which is said to be so unusual that they suspect it is not a primate at all, but a species of giant sloth.

Nevertheless, lurking in the background are native legends of mysterious animals which really do sound like southern versions of the northern bigfoot. First hand reports are rather difficult to come by, so we might as well look at the few we have.

Chapter 7

Honduras: Encounter in a Dark Hut

This time no translation is necessary, for the story comes from the English language monthly, *The Wide World Magazine*, which ran from 1898 to 1965 - late enough to come to my attention during my boyhood. I have since attempted to acquire any copy available at the right price.

The journal, it is important to explain, was designed as a forum for people to relate their true life adventures. Each story submitted was required to be accompanied by a written statement that it was original and strictly true in all particulars, and I suspect that this was generally the case. Most of them do not have the beginning, middle, and end typical of fiction. Nevertheless, hoaxes and stories strongly suspected of being hoaxes were known to have crept in. For what it is worth, it appears that, at least up to the 1930s, payment at an unspecified level was made for stories. That certainly wasn't the case from the 1940s onwards, when the editor got his material gratis.

Be that as it may, this chapter is taken from:

"The Gold-Seekers",
told by Edward J. Hoyt, and set down by Dr. Vance Hoyt,
The Wide World Magazine, vol. 34, no. 205 (May 1915), pp 3 -16.[30]

The plot of the story - if that's the right word - was straightforward. The author was one of a group of Americans who, in 1898, decided to seek their fortune looking for gold in Honduras. Accompanied by a guide and a caravan of pack animals, they departed Trujillo for the mountains and dense jungles of the interior. After about a month, at a place called Viajo, they sold their pack animals and hired carriers for a journey of about fifty miles to the region of the Julan River, where they prospected for gold for several years, until driven out by political chicanery and a gun fight. It is important to note that the cryptozoological incident was only one of several adventures they experienced on the way, and not the focus of the story. I would a have been seriously suspicious of any story entitled (say) "I fought the monster of Honduras" or "Encounter in a dark hut."

---

[30] You can read the whole issue at
https://archive.org/details/TheWideWorldUSV035N205191505

Shortly before their arrival at Viajo they made the mistake, as can be judged by hindsight, of camping on a wildlife trail in the jungle. In the middle of the night a couple of wild beasts blundered into their camp, resulting in pandemonium, which ended with their guide being trampled to death, and one of the animals being shot.

> It was about the size of a donkey - a pig-like mammal, having a short proboscis, and a most peculiar and ferocious-looking head. Its hide was thick and tough, its feet three-toed, its ears like those of a burro, and its tail like that of a mule.

He said they were dreaded by all those who travel in the interior because of their attacks on wayfarers. They often demolish the fields of corn planted in clearings in the forest, and they travel at night along special trails.

It is perfectly clear that this was a *danta*, or Baird's tapir, *Tapirus bairdii*, and was correctly illustrated as such by the magazine artist. The only error in the description was the tail like a mule's. It has three toes on the hind foot, and four on the forefoot. The interesting thing is that neither the author, nor the relative who ghost-wrote his account, knew that.

> I do not know the scientific name for this creature, if there is one, but the natives call it the "Danto".

This is important because, if a writer can be shown to have accurately described something unknown to him, we can be more confident of his accuracy when describing something unknown to all of us. So let us now proceed to the crucial encounter with cryptid which, as far as I can establish, occurred about half way between the start of the journey and the adventure with the tapir. I shall now take you to the text on pp 6 to 8 of the magazine.

. . . .

Making steady progress, we camped a few days later in a low, thickly-wooded valley surrounded on all sides by mountains. Just before sundown I discovered an old deserted cabin close to the range to the south of us. I proposed that we should sleep in it that night, but the *mozo* [guide] warned me to keep away from the place. There was a "devil" in the hut, he said.

I tried to urge some of our party to go with me, but they all agreed that where the guide slept was good enough for them. They said it was not good judgment to take risks that even a native declined. Having a determined disposition this made me stubborn; I determined to sleep in that hut or know the reason why.

Again I questioned the *mozo* about the old adobe. All he knew was that the place, according to all accounts, had not been inhabited for close on sixty years. Stray natives had slept upon its floor, but before daybreak they had been roughly handled by some powerful "thing", and in most cases terribly mutilated. No one had tried to discover what this dread "thing" was, and now everyone passed the cabin at a distance, muttering to themselves, "Mucho diablo."

"Well, if there is a devil in there I am going to make his acquaintance," I said; and I got up from the camp fire and began to examine my revolver to satisfy myself that every chamber was loaded.

Alamondo [the guide] fell on his knees before me and began to mutter a short prayer. As I was buckling on my cartridge-belt he begged me to tie a little red sack he held in his hand around my neck, which, he said, would keep the "devil" away. Not taking the trouble to examine what it contained, I did as he said. These natives are like children, and in order to keep them faithful to you it is best to please them as much as possible. Then, bidding the others good night, I took up my blanket and made for the cabin.

After having some trouble in opening the old door, I found myself in a low, musty-smelling room, which looked as if it had not been occupied since the days of Noah. I took a candle from my belt, lit it, and began to investigate a little.

The floor consisted of split logs, full of holes, laid across old sleepers. The whole cabin, in fact, was built of split logs, plastered over with mud. In the north wall there was a large niche between the logs, evidently meant for a window. Just under this was an old bunk, and this I decided should be my resting-place for the night.

I was satisfied with my lodging, so I blew out he candle. As I did so I looked through the niche in the wall, and saw the *mozo* building a huge camp fire, which is the custom of these natives to keep wild animals from bothering them.

Stretching my weary limbs, I wrapped my blanket around me and was soon lost to the world.

I do not know how long I slept, but it must have been after midnight when I was suddenly awakened by the sound of something or someone walking on the loose planks of the floor. I slowly reached down my side and gripped the butt of my Colt, my finger encircling the trigger, ready for action. I was not to be taken by surprise, and breathlessly awaited the intruder's first move.

The noise continued at the farther side of the room, but it now seemed to be more along the side of the wall than on the floor. I was puzzled to know what it could be. It did not sound like an animal; the thing walked like a man, for I could only hear the tread of two feet.

Slowly and carefully I drew myself up until I rested on the elbow of my left arm. I peered into the darkness towards the opposite side of the room. I stared and stared until my eyes ached, and then, all of a sudden, I heard the heavy breathing of something almost directly above me. Look up quickly, I saw two red eyes, like balls of fire, staring down at me.

I was levelling my revolver, when, without warning, my blanket began to slowly slide from my grasp. Something was climbing up over the foot of my bunk! I turned my my head quickly. Two red eyes stared at my - directly in front.

Then I pulled the trigger, and my faithful revolver sputtered lead.

It would be impossible for me to try to describe what happened after that, for I do not know myself. I only know that the most hideous shrieks and screams a human being ever heard grated on my ears; there was a rush, a scramble; and then something sprang over my head and out through the large niche in the wall. I could hear the cracking of bushes outside as it swept up the side of the mountain.

I sprang up and looked out of the window to see if I could discover what I had hit, and saw the rest of the party, guns in hand, running towards me. The *mozo*, after stirring the camp fire, had lit a pitch-pine knot and was following in the rear.

I opened the door, and by the aid of the flaring torch we saw something furry lying at the foot of my bunk. I was stooping down to examine it, when Alamondo caught my arm and jumped back in fright.

"No, no, Don José!" he shrieked. "Come away! Come away! Halingo! Halingo!"

With my foot I turned the animal over, and convinced the frightened guide that it was dead.

I had never seen such a creature before. It stood about five feet high, evidently belonged to the ape family, and resembled a man more than anything else. These animals are of a brownish colour except their faces, which are white. They walk erect on their hind feet, and the males possess a long white beard, which gives them a very peculiar appearance. The female carries her young in her arms, the same as a woman. The interior of Central America is their habitat; I do not know of any other jungles in which they are found. They are seldom seen in the day-time, are very ferocious when cornered, and have enough muscular strength to outmatch a dozen men. The natives call this remarkable man-monkey the "Halingo," and regard it as an evil spirit.

. . . .

Remember: he was writing almost 17 years after the events, so his recall of the exact sequence of events may be defective. However, if it is accurate, then it would appear that two of the creatures entered via the "window", the first without wakening him until it was inside. For what it is worth, he provided a photograph of the hut, but not the carcass. Be that as it may, it is clear that he received most of the information on their habits from the local inhabitants. He appears to regard the "halingo" in the same light as the "danto": as a representative of the local fauna known to the inhabitants, but not to him. But what was it?

My first guess was some sort of large monkey. The white-fronted spider monkey, *Ateles belzebuth* was almost certainly the species behind the Loy's ape hoax. Stretched out, a big specimen may well reach four feet from heel to crown. Unfortunately, it lives in South America, not Central America. Also, it does not fit the description. There are only three (official) species of monkeys in Honduras: a spider monkey, a howler, and a capuchin, and none of them is anywhere as large or looks anything like the "halingo". Admittedly, I am not completely conversant with all the New World monkeys, but I can't think of any of them - at least no large one - which possesses a long white beard. Also, although the author did not actually say it was tailless, he implied it. I doubt that, even illuminated only with a flaming torch, the long, thick, prehensile tail of these primates would have been overlooked.

Not only that, but I doubt if any of the locals would have described any New World primate as bipedal. There is another thing: American primates are arboreal, diurnal, and predominantly gregarious. You really don't expect a couple of any known species to be lurking around a deserted cabin at night. It is noteworthy, however, that just about all the mystery apes around the world are alleged to be predominantly nocturnal and solitary. Students of bigfootery, furthermore, will be aware that these creatures are reported almost everywhere, and in Central America they are called *sisimite* and *xipe*. Perhaps we can now add *halingo* to the list of synonyms.

Chapter 8

Ape Attack in Guatemala

Dorion, R. C. (1963). Mono apareció por tierras de Izabal.
(An ape appeared in the grounds of Izabal),   *Genus* 19:163-5

Mr. ROBERT C. DORION
of Guatemala communicates the following information, published on 12
December 1962 by the daily *La Prensa Libre* of Guatemala.[31]

Ape appeared in the grounds of Izabal

HAIRRAISING ADVENTURE LIVED BY HUNTERS: MONSTROUS ANIMAL MORE THAN TWO METRES TALL.

At the point of losing their lives, in the hands of what they considered an anthropoid of gigantic size, four hunters thus found themselves when they entered the mountain area of the Irayoles, situated between the village of Juan de Paz, of the municipality of Los Amantes and Lake Izabal, at being surprised by the said beast when they were sleeping peacefully.

The leader of the expedition was Mr. Tomás Morales, resident of the village of Juan de Paz, and on Monday 3 of the current month [ie December 1962], at an early hour - accompanied by three other hunters from the region - he entered the mountain area.

The whole of the day was dedicated to the hunt. Two of them went armed with their respective rifles of calibre 22 and the others with work machetes. When the night came down, they got ready to sleep in the part of the mountain known as Tipón Volcano, and after having prepared the meals, organized turns at standing watch for whatever might happen. Morales and another of his companions had the first watch until 12 o'clock at night, seated at the edge of a fire.

At 12 o'clock, they awoke their travelling companions and instructed them to maintain the blaze and to be alert, because during the period of the watch they had heard strange noises of something moving around nervously in the undergrowth, breaking dry bushes as it travelled.

---

[31] For some reason, this sentence is in French, while everything else is in Spanish.

Morales and his companion fell asleep immediately. They were so tired they could scarcely hold their eyes open for a few minutes. Nevertheless, those charged with the second watch did not comply well with their commission. They did not poke the blaze, and soon fell asleep.

A NIGHTMARE

Moments later absolute silence reigned, when the four hunters slept. The fire went out. They woke up when they heard some cries nearby. Morales and his first turn companion were suddenly held fast by two powerful arms, heavily covered with hair. Both were being lifting into the air. Morales remained between the chest of the horrible, hairy beast which, with an enormous hand [obscure] his mouth, and his other companion was seized by the waist. The beast intended to take them into the interior of the forest.

The second turn companions woke up immediately and fired at the gigantic beast - of some two metres eighty centimetres [9ft 2 in], as Mr José Lino Accituno reported - 18 shots in total, but without any effective result. Probably the thickness of the skin and the quantity of hair which covered it deadened the impacts.

SOLE RECOURSE: THE FIRE

One of those who were being made prisoner by the anthropoid and whose mouth remained free, let out fearful cries. He was trying to retrieve the matches from his purse, but was unable to do so, as long as the beast was slowly travelling towards the interior of the forest. Suddenly he succeeded in crying out that they should try to set fire to the thick mantle of hair which covered it, and one of them approached and did so.

The hair of the strange, enormous animal began to burn like tinder. When it felt that its hair was burning, it let go of its two victims and hurried off, like a torch, into the forest.

STRANGE INDIVIDUAL

The four hunters, when they had got over the terror, set out to return to the village. Morales and his companions in adventure came out of it with slight knocks and bruises, as a consequence of the strong pressure which the beast exerted against their bodies.

They took their implements and got out of that ominous place.

As described by Mr Aceltuno, a labourer of the road to the Atlantic, Mr Morales has reported that he is dealing with a strange individual.

They consider that when [obscure] it measures two metres eighty centimetres. Its hands are broad, its fingers especially bulky. Likewise is lower extremities.

It has been informed that the authorities of that department have not been advised of the presence of this strange animal, so they suggest an expedition in order to attempt to locate it. Besides, it is believed that there exist more individuals of this species.

Chapter 9

Bigfoot in the Andes

The author of the following essay, written in 1963, was a journalist for *El Tribuno*, the newspaper of the province of Salta, tucked into the far northwest corner of Argentina. It thus includes the foothills of the Andes, although he cites legends from farther afield. As I mentioned before, bigfoot-type rumours are not unknown in South America, and the author apparently accepts this identity. Just the same, the description of the animal is extremely limited. All that one can say is that one would expect the average peasant to be able to recognize a bear, even an unknown species. Also, the behaviour of running away with its hands clutched to its head doesn't sound too ursine to me!

I apologize in advance for the text. The author's form of literary Spanish tends to convert to a rather stilted English, but I have chosen to sacrifice style in favour of accuracy. Even in regard to the latter, problems arise. Firstly, my Spanish is only passable. Secondly, every word in a language bears a variety of meanings and connotations which do not transfer exactly into a second language. Thirdly, this essay contains a number of dialectal terms and slang absent from even the best dictionaries. Nevertheless, though I am prepared to accept criticism of specific words and phrases, I believe the overall meaning of the text has been preserved.

. . . .

Milenko Juan Jurcich (1963): Tarma, el hombre salvaje de América. (Tarma, the wild man of America) *Genus* 19: pp 166-174

When the mountaineers began the siege of the peak of Everest, there ran through the world, especially in the scientific media, a species of astonishment and incredulity, before the news that these mountain climbers were about to accomplish their expeditions.

It was said to be an animal species of enormous stature. These first news items were made known by Captain J. B. Noel, who was in the Himalayas in the year 1926. Noel states in his book, *Through Tibet*: "There is near the monastery a fascinating legend in which all good Tibetans believe and which refers to the Nikitkanjis or "Snowmen". This is the name which the Lamas give it, because they are frightful beings which live in the snow."

Later on, Noel added: "The Tibetan peasant calls these beings SUKPA and speaks of their strange ramblings on the snow and their long head hair, which falls over the eyes ..." Soon, the mountaineer photographer wondered: "What are these beings: men, apes, bears? No-one could say. But there must be some background to this legend, which is already considered an accepted fact in those valleys of Tibet."

For those interested in the question of the "Abominable Snowman", it is not necessary to collect further antecedents. On the other hand, much data of no less interest was being collected by those initially speaking about the appearance of the Yeti in those Asiatic regions.

As an Andeanist, fan of archaeology, and a journalist, I was no less interested in this new unknown appearing in the middle of the Asian continent. Just the same, when, in this part of America there were said to be weak traces remaining in the past which very much resembled it, where it had produced the extraordinary event, it then raised up an particular enthusiasm to accumulate the numerous and interesting experiences, which did not cease to erase my doubts on the origin of those analogous particularities of both continents to the extent that I could reach a final, narrow conclusion, without of course making up my mind to establish what would be the original point, but inclining me to this: that it was the American continent.

> He then goes on for a couple of pages discussing questionable theories about links between Central Asia and South America.

Captain Noel says that the Tibetan peasant calls these beings Sukpa and alludes to the rare custom which that mysterious personage has of stealing their women[32]

In the central part of South America, especially in Paraguay, the legend also coincides with the analogous terminology, because it is said and believed that Zupay also steal women with whom they are in love, and thus it it held in the popular consensus that persons with reddish hair are born to women whom Zupai fall in love with, in some corner of the Guaraní forest.

Now then, the legend also draws from the past the physical traces of Zukpa Zupay. Both, according to those references, are beings of

---

[32] He is unaware that *pa* in Tibetan means "a people" e.g. Sherpa = "east people", and that many societies accuse great apes of carrying off women.

enormous height and of reddish hair which completely covers the body. As one will be able to infer, it would only be sufficient to place both legendary personages face to face in order to turn it into crude reality when it is today only a mystery and legend.

For the Salteño mountains [ie the mountains of Salta], Zupay is the Ukumar, bear man, of enormous physical frame, which used to dominate the forest zones and the pre-Andes ranges, which today bear the denomination of the Metán and Lerma Valleys. The Ukumar appeared on repeated occasions to the populations of Esteco, the first capital of the Argentine north and the province of Salta, which was swallowed by the earth after the violent earthquakes of 1692.

The Ukomar appeared with his enormous, reddish, hairy presence to the coaches which used to pass *en route* to Charcas and Peru. The last references to the Ukumar has survived, by strange circumstances, in that region of the Andean spurs where no-one ventures. It is said to have found refuge, hurried and perhaps harassed, secure in the chain of mountains entangled with virgin forest. This brings to memory the expressions of the Duke of Argyll: "that the savage races which still subsist in the world, are simple exiles of the human species descending from weak, rejected tribes to the woods and crags."

But the Ukumar and the Zupay are not the only wild beings of which references reach us through the legend. We also have that of the Tupay, which joins and brings all of its analogy to those already mentioned.

The Spanish navigator Pedro Sarmiento de Gamboa, in the second part of his *General History Called Indian*, speaks of those elderly Aymara Indians brought together to relate to him all that they knew of the past and of the Inca Empire, and stood out as using a word with the denomination of a "wild man". This word is Tarma. Around Cuzco there exists in the present day a population which bears that strange denomination, which in the era of the Aymaras was given to a mysterious wild man.

Who was Tarma? Where did he live? Whence did he arise?

Many are the questions which we can put to ourselves about this word, which opens such a tremendous query, more, it is much less than we can know intuitively. We have no knowledge, at present, of the works undertaken in that respect, nor other references than those made by the Spanish sailor.

The legends, customs, and the other analogies which tightly link the Asian and American continents do not succeed, however, in relieving us of the uncertainty of which comes from which.

He then argues that the first syllable of *tar-ma* and the last syllable of the Tibetan *yeh-teh* and *mi-teh* are cognates, and both mean "wild man".

No more than 40 years ago, the gauchos did not venture much to penetrate into the dense forest or leave for zones which the human footstep would seldom tread, for fear of confronting the terrible Ukumar. The Jesuits who used to work in the tunnels of gold and silver of Cerro Crestón, 3820 metres hight, in the Valley of Uetán, Salta, used to hastily withdraw to their ranches, not long before sunset for fear of an encounter with the bear man.

Little by little the legend was being lost. The advance of civilisation was, perhaps, displacing the surprising animal man, of which very little is spoken with the exception of the hamlets penetrated deepest into the countryside. However, one evening in 1956, there arrived at the editorial office of *El Tribuno*, a simple man who then revealed that he had been working with some American engineers in Metá. These had arrived in that zone in order to locate and study the works which the Jesuits made and which consisted of a tunnel which crossed below the voluminous Juramento River and permitted the passage of coaches and passengers towards Old Peru in colonial times.

According to references obtained by another channel and totally unconnected with that which the simple visitor offered, those engineers were no other than the ones who constructed the famous dam at Boulder City. [That would have been 20 years before.]

The informant gave me a lot of data on the strange apparition of which he was a personal witness and of the enormous interest in the Americans in hunting the huge reddish bear that had appeared to them. I took his name and his declarations and stored them among the motley collection of notes and papers on my desk. Time passed, and with the transfer of the newspaper's building, a "clean-up operation" was performed, and it was swept away with those papers and notes which would be of much value to me today. However, because of the interest that fact awoke in me, which immediately established ties with the Yeti of the Himalayas, that circumstance has remained engraved in my mind, if not the name of the worker.

Some years later, in different circumstances, I began to run into a rare version of the appearance of the Ukumar in mountainous, heavily vegetated zones. As the same had gained a large diffusion and there also had arrived numerous correspondence to the editing of the daily, the management charged me with the initiation of a series of references which I faced in an indirect manner, and without discounting the possibility of its existence, publishing on the other hand a very narrow synthesis of the tale which the worker had given.

The unknown which surrounded the Ukumar remained latent to the readers throughout those publications, and then refreshed the memory of the old inhabitants who wrote to us recounting astonishing facts and strange occurrences of many years before. I myself reached the stage of asking myself whether or not the Ukumar might exist. If his prodigious figure might still be strolling through the Chaco forests.

Many letters arrived and almost all were thrown away, but the surprise had no limits when the correspondent in the neighbouring locality of Chicoana raised the alert.

It was reported to us that the town had a valley muleteer who insisted that he had encountered the Ukumar and that he had also been given the pleasure of shooting him with his old shotgun.

In one of the many crossings which the same had made towards this town in quest of trade goods, our correspondent interviewed the peasant. He was revealed to be a native of the Escoipe Gorge, situated to the west of the Lerma Valley where there is a lot of mountainous country covered with thick vegetation and which abounds in sachaceibos[33], cochuchos and other trees more than 50 metres high.

Ciriaco Taritolay, 65 years old, burly and hardened by the Andean cold, was still riding with the same grace and security of his early years. Of clear intelligence and very [uncertain] in speech to develop the rare philosophy of the country man, he revealed himself to be a man well experienced in confronting danger.

The account which we rendered in the daily was done in the presence of the correspondent, the neighbour Pablo Vega and of numerous friends and parrishioners of the town.The hair raising tale came to life, as he explained it, on the stretch of road which goes from Pulares to the mountain, where there is a zone of thick vegetation. Very

---

[33] probably the coral tree

close to the latter, for several years, there lie some archaeological ruins of great importance in Peñas Azules.

It came as no surprise, then, that right from his entrance Don Ciriaco Taritolay would express in the particular manner of the country man, that left no place for doubt: "I know that the Ukumar exists" in order to take up his story.

[Don Ciriaco takes up the story.] My beasts [unclear] saw him, so the "varmint" didn't take me by surprise. But he did not get a julep flower with his rare appearance. This was some days before, when I came to the town and entered the site of Agua Chulla. It was cloudy. You know that, at sunset, the hill is cloaked with clouds. I came, as is my custom, well strung with gear to lower onto the pack donkeys which would follow later on. Soon, when they left, they were running scared in all directions and downhill. In the face of this inopportune behaviour of the animals, I [unclear, but it seems he attempted to restrain the lead animal.] My first thought was on the possible presence of a rattlesnake or coral snake on the path, but while I was trying to find the crawling varmints in the verdant undergrowth, I got a strange feeling.

It was a rare feeling, as if someone was looking at me. I did not feel the cold of the damp foothills so much as the shudder which ran through my body when I quickly lifted my sight right towards that "something" which was present. Among the undergrowth and taking with his broad, hairy arms between two bulky sachaceibos, stood looking curiously at me, as if looking from within, a frightful being.

I believe that I perhaps said frightful because of the unforeseen form which appeared to me, and because it was unexpected. Now I think that it had something of the playful varmint more than anything, in spite of its tremendous girth. As I told them, I knew of the Ukumar but never thought that the self-same creature would present itself to me in flesh and bone, and even less in those places where I only encounter foxes, viscachas and other small animals.

I remained paralysed, [unclear] strongly to my [?] lead animal, which was also snorting, knowing intuitively the danger which we were facing, and it was pulling on the bridle, kicking, and backing up. I did not know if the rare animal which held itself erect was at least thinking to attack me or if it would remain there the whole afternoon looking at me. It required just a moment to take out my "blunderbuss" from its sleeve and aiming it roughly, because my animal was still unsettled, to raise it, aiming between the two trees, and fire a tremendous blast.

A treacherous yell escaped from the toothy mouth and, grasping its head with both hands, it lost itself at once in the density of the wood. The "varmint" would have been more than two metres [6 ft 7 in] high, and completely covered with medium red [unclear] hair, and of a tremendous strength that I calculate that if it brought its arms together it would have broken the trees."

This was approximately the report of Don Ciriaco Taritolay who, since that day, left the trail which used to shorten by half the crossing to the locality of Chicoana to San Fernando de Escoipe. Now he takes the route which follows the ravine of the noisy Escoipe River, which issues violently from the heights of the Cerro Negro. This occurred in the middle of June 1956.

These appearances, as far as I know, have been produced regularly and in different forms, however by rare mythological analogy, until today. Just like the strange animal of Tibet, the mysterious American being, it has not been able to be hunted in order to finally elucidate that unknown which the Aymaras believe in as Tarma, their "wild man".

PART IV

AFRICA

Africa has no bigfoots, but it does have its share of littlefoots and mediumfoots. In other words, there are rumours of unknown primates which are not simply variations on a theme.

Some, of course, are variations on a known theme. Thus, towards the end of the last century, in the Bili Forest of the Democratic Republic of the Congo, the Bili apes, or Bondo apes were discovered: a subspecies of big chimpanzees which act a lot like gorillas - indeed, not unlike the "mangani" of the Tarzan novels. Then there is the *koolookamba*, whose existence is fairly well established, but whose identity is not. It is likely it is a separate species of chimpanzee which is moving towards extinction. (Another reason why cryptozoology is an important discipline.)

In his seminal work, *On the Track of Unknown Animals,* Dr Heuvelmans made mention of reports of "little hairy men" in various parts of the continent, and referred them to *Australopithecus africanus*, a fossil species close to the base of the human family tree. Since then, a large number of branches of this family tree have been discovered in Africa, providing a wide range of possible identities for any mystery primate which might turn up.

Not only that, but throughout the African savanna belt there exist legends of races of small humans as the original inhabitants of the land before the ancestors of the current inhabitants arrived. There is almost certainly a lot of truth in these legends, because, with the development of agriculture and animal husbandry, the farming and pastoral tribes expanded, absorbing, destroying, or pushing aside those which still relied on hunting and gathering. Not all the hunter gatherers were small, of course, but many were. Their last representatives are the Pygmies of the Equatorial forest, who now live in a symbiotic relationship with the agricultural tribes, and the Bushmen of southern Africa, who occupy land nobody else wants.

Approximately 70,000 years ago, *Homo sapiens* migrated out of Africa to settle the rest of the world. But long before that, two major splits occurred in the human lineage. The first led to the Bushmen, the most ancient of all the divisions of mankind, followed by the Pygmies, the second most ancient. The rest of the black Africans represent the third, and everybody else the fourth. But not everything is as it seems - as the first chapter in this section will reveal.

Chapter 10

Unknown African Pygmies?

As mentioned before, Africa abounds in legends of a race of pygmies which preceded the current inhabitants, and the legends may be based on fact. But the following article involves the possible current existence of such pygmies - humans, not animals - in the savanna woodlands of the Central African Republic (CAR). As French is the official language of the CAR, I have retained the French spellings of place names, but have transcribed the native word, *toulou* into the more English, *tulu* - though perhaps *tooloo* would be more appropriate. Unfortunately, like the other writers for *Bipedia*, the author labels all bipedal mystery primates "hominians" - which leads to a regrettable confusion with the term, "Homininae", the scientific term for mankind and its closest relatives. Nevertheless, I have retained the term, in the absence of any alternative.

The summary of the original article is in English, and I have left it as is. The rest is in French, and once more, I have sought accuracy rather than elegance.

. . . .

Christian le Noël (1960), Recherches sur des hominiens inconnus de République Centrafricaine   (Research on Unknown Hominians of the Central African Republic)   *Bipedia* 4: 11-15 (March 1990)

SUMMARY : Certain hominians, still unknown, may have survived in Africa : traditions, especially in Central Africa, speak of " bush-dwarfs " who live in really out-of-the-way places. They are described as being small, about as tall as a young boy of ten or eleven, stocky, very vigorous and dark-skinned; they have their own language, they make their own natural weapons and they wear skirts made of hide, but nevertheless they don't build any permanent abodes; they live on berries and wild honey. The legend goes that they captivate the will of any casual passers-by, taking them prisoner and releasing them later after a teach [sic] about how to cure themselves by plants. All known descriptions agree on this point, and there is not one which gives the lie to the others: everything seems to fit in. The vernacular languages all have precise words to describe these dwarfs: some of these words which are used to mention the dwarfs are also used to describe the surrounding natural phenomena such as hills and caves. There were allegedly many more of these dwarfs in the past than there are now, the Bantus used them as carriers, or killed them as game, according to the testimony of a Portuguese navigator of the 16th century.

The author has personally pieced together two different accounts, one from Oumar Boukar, a 50 years old Arab businessman, who claimed to have met one of these bush-dwarfs in 1965, while he was hunting and he found himself separated from his companions; the other testimony comes from a missionary father from Yppi who thought he had met a little boy belonging to one of his fellow tribesman, but was in fact a bush-dwarf: the latter almost broke his bones while shaking hands. In the same regions, cupules cut out in the rocks by human hands were also found. The author of this text also discovered newly made foot-prints of very small size, at a distance much too far away from the villages to suppose that they were made by a child.

These bush-dwarfs may well be descendants of the Koïsan lineage; the same identical evidence has been reported from Kenya, and yet Kenya is by no means near Central Africa. Certain ethnologists have not counted out the fact of a possible survive [sic] by certain primitive races in the very place where they first appeared

The native inhabitants of this area are familiar with certain caves which are supposed to be or to have been the refuge of bush-dwarfs, as well as dozens of burial mounds, made of nodules of laterite, which are incomprehensible to everybody. Finally in the prefecture of La Lobaye in 1988, hunters shot down a creature which was so strange that they dared not eat it, and they brought it to the chief of police who had it buried on the spot. A report was sent to the head of the state who wrote in the margin in his hand-writing the following comment: "A pity as far as science is concerned".

Translation

At the dawn of the 21st century, there still remain shadow zones in which belong the races of hominians which have peopled, or which perhaps still people, certain areas of our planet.

Africa is, along with Asia, the continent where tradition, legends, and sometimes testimonies, speak of apparently unknown hominians having lived, or still living, in certain regions less populated because of difficulty of access. In Central Africa, for example, the tradition speaks of "bush dwarfs": types of savanna pygmies, of which some representatives perhaps still survive in our days in the regions of the northeast. From the descriptions which the natives make, these "bush dwarfs" would be as tall as a ten year old child, and would be very squat and of great strength. Their complexion would be black. They speak, they possess hunting weapons, and skirts of hide, but do not construct huts or any habitation.

If one believes the tradition, these beings especially frequent the woody and rocky places of the Sudano-Guinean savanna. They feed on roots, berries, and wild honey. In these descriptions the natives all agree that the bush dwarfs would have the power to take away the will of a man whom chance places in their road in the isolated districts of the bush; they could thus compel a man to follow them for some time, in order to afterwards restore his mental freedom. The one who thus makes a forced sojourn with the "bush dwarfs" often returns home with knowledge of the art of healing by means of plants. In the different regions of the CAR, this description is always the same. On the other hand, each vernacular language possesses a specific name to designate the "bush dwarfs"; the Bandas name them "Kara-Komba", literally "the apes who carry a lot", an allusion to their strength and also to the fact that they have without doubt been employed in carrying. The Arabs in the northern region call them "Dam-Sako", but there exists also a generic term which one finds throughout the territory, ie the name, *Tulu* or *Tulé*, or again, *Tollé*, depending on the tribe. This term is also found in place names in certain regions: there exists a "Tulu" river; there is also a "Tulu" rock shelter, and a "Tulu" Kaga, or hill.

According to tradition, there was a distant era when the bush dwarfs were relatively numerous, and the Bantu employed them at crude tasks, like carrying. Apparently, they were considered as game and eaten, as witnesses in the account of the voyage of a Portuguese navigator of the 16th century, who related having been present, in what is now Burkina Faso, in a chase with dogs, in which an entire family of "bush dwarfs" was cut down by the natives of the place, who carried out a beat to obtain meat.

Testimonies of meetings between bush dwarfs and natives are not very rare. I have collected two which seem worthy of belief. The first was in the northern district, for the mouth of a local Arab businessman:

"My name is Oumar Boukar. I am 50 years old. In 1965 I
was diamond prospecting in the district of Ouadda. With nine
companions, we had left on the trail from Pata, to the heights

of the village of Tchanga. We intended to procure meat by hunting. We were following the fresh spoor of an antelope which had just crossed the trail, when at a certain moment, the vegetation became quite dense and I found myself isolated from my companions. Suddenly, in the middle of the thicket, I found myself in the presence of a "bush dwarf", which we call *'Dam-Sako'*. He was about 1 m 10 *[3 ft 7 in]* high, but his body was very broad. He carried a little axe on his back, he was dressed in a pubic apron *[cache-sexe]* of animal skin, and something like a pair of crude sandals. He was black with a shaved skull. He resembled a black man, but with the stature of a child. I tried to seize him and take him in my arms; he began to let out dull, incomprehensible cry. He got free of my grip very easily, and disappeared into the surrounding vegetation. At that precise moment, my head started to spin, and I completely lost my sense of direction. I remained without moving, and began to say my prayers, for I am a Moslem. I was so ill at ease I believed my last hour had come. At the end of a moment, I heard in the distance my companions calling for me. I replied, and was soon reunited with them. The *'Dam-Sako'* are quite numerous in this region, but one meets them very rarely, because they hide from man."

This testimony was collected courtesy of Brother Pierre of the Catholic mission at Ndélé. The second testimony is an adventure which happened to a missionary father of Yppi; it was reported to me by Father Fischer of the Catholic mission at Birao.

One of the fathers at the Yppi mission was in the habit of greeting all the natives he met on the bush trails. One day, when he was driving around in a 2CV[34] on one of these little trails linking two hamlets, he noticed what he took for a little boy. He slowed down to his height and greeting him in the local language. Receiving no reply, he stopped his vehicle a little farther on and got out to talk to the stranger, all the time tendering his hand. The stranger seized and gripped it so strongly that the good Father felt it was being squeezed in a vice. As he recounted his adventure on his return to the mission, the natives laughingly told him that he had without doubt met a "bush dwarf", who have a reputation for strength! It would have been interesting to question this missionary

---

[34] A small French automobile produced by Citroën

father who, to my knowledge, is perhaps one of the rare Europeans to have seen at close range one of the famous "*Kara-Komba*", spoken of by the blacks in this part of the CAR.

Throughout the territory, one can discover on the rocky outcrops little cup-like receptacles about 5.5 to 6 cm [2 in] in diameter. The blacks claim that these are traces left by *Tulu"*, in order to build their house! These cups are visibly hollowed by the hand of man; in general they come in twos or fours, 20 to 30 centimetres [8 to 12 in] apart. What could be their use? I have seen the same thing in the district of St. Étienne in France.

I personally have twice been in the presence of fresh footprints in very isolated regions, where there was no village less than a hundred kilometres away. These footprints were visibly prints of human beings, but of a very small height, like those of a little boy. Now, there is no way a child could survive alone more than a hundred kilometres from any village! In these inhospitable regions, the natives move around only in groups. These footprints were no more than about 15 to 18 centimetres [6 to 7 inches] long, and the strides did not exceed 50 cm [20 in].

What can these bush dwarfs be? Perhaps distant relict descendants of the *Khoisan* race, whose rock paintings have come down to us. It might be that some of them would also have been present in the wooded regions of Kenya. There also, recent native testimonies speak of *bush dwarfs*. Let's listen to the description which was made of one of them: "Its eyes, its mouth, were those of a man, and its face was not covered with hair, but its brow was very low, rather like that of a baboon." Those were the terms by which a Kenyan described the strange creature he had encountered one day, when he was hunting in the forest, and by which he had been held prisoner for more than an hour.

It is to be noted that Kenya is several thousand kilometres away from the CAR, and that this testimony does not seem to be able to have been influenced by the identical accounts of that country. These testimonies have convinced one French sociologist, Jacqueline ROUMEGUERRE-EBERHARDT, research master at the CNRS, that the hominians known up to then by their fossil remains, are perhaps still living in Kenya (1,2,3). Why then, wonders Mrs Roumeguèrre-Eberhardt, might not *Homo habilis* and *Homo erectus*, which lived 500,000 to 3 million years ago, still be alive in this region where they first appeared?

This theory might be confirmed by the fact that the climatology of these regions has apparently changed little since distant times, at least in the proportions, extreme variations of which would have caused a well-adapted species to disappear. For example, in the CAR, where I carried out the research on the bush dwarfs, I have noticed that the region most rich in testimonies was a region where a fossil plant, the *Encephalartos* still grows. This plant used to exist 20 to 30 million years ago, a contemporary of the famous dinosaurs [!][35] It is a sort of large, spiny fern. If this plant has resisted the present climate, why not a race of hominians?

For my part, the natives' descriptions of these bush dwarfs make me think of those made by the Breton legends describing the *Korrigans* and the farfardets, who also were of small stature and had the power to take away the will of their victims in order to make them do whatever passed in their heads.

In the region of Bamingui there was discovered a cave on a "Kaga", in which were shut up three unknown skeletons; a thorough study would be necessary to identify exactly the origin and exact nature of these three skeletons, whose manner of burial is unknown in this region. When interrogated, the natives claimed that these human remains dated from before the arrival of their ancestors into the country. In the region of Bamingui, where testimonies on the bush dwarfs are numerous, the professional guide, Alain MOUSIST discovered, in February 1988, in a cave of the Goumbiri River, some rock paintings. It is the first time such paintings have been discovered in the CAR, where until now only engravings have turned up.

Relief of rock paintings in a cave in the region of Bamingui.
People with what appears to be a monitor lizard.

---

[35] The dinosaurs became extinct 66 million years ago, but *Encephalartos* is a genus of cycads, and is much older than the dinosaurs

A little to the north, in the chain of hills which dominate the valley of the Aouk River, there also exists a series of caves and cavities hollowed out by rain water in the sole limestone site in the country (several hundreds of square kilometres!). The natives of the neighbouring villages claim that these caves serve as refuges for the bush dwarf's, and that at certain times they can hear music issuing from these caves, which are practically inaccessible, for they are full of wild beehives; the African bees being particularly aggressive, it is difficult to penetrate into those rocky holes

One last mystery needs to be clarified in this region. There exist thousands of piles of laterite nodules, visibly built by the hand of man. There also, no native is capable of saying what used could be the little tumuli of about a metre cube. They are content to say: "There were people before us who made these, before our parents." It is very difficult to open these tumuli, for the laterite nodules are fused over time to form a block as hard as concrete.

The archaeologist, P. VIDAL, who undertakes research for CNRS in the region of Bouar on the megaliths, passed through this region and discovered a skeleton in the the shelter of Tulu on the Ndélé-Birao track, the skeleton of a normal man dated by C_{14} to 400 years.

In 1986, a strange event occurred in the prefecture of la Lobaye: local African hunters, going into the forest, felled a being which they had initially taken for a big monkey, but which so strongly resembled a human being that they did not dare to carve it up to eat.

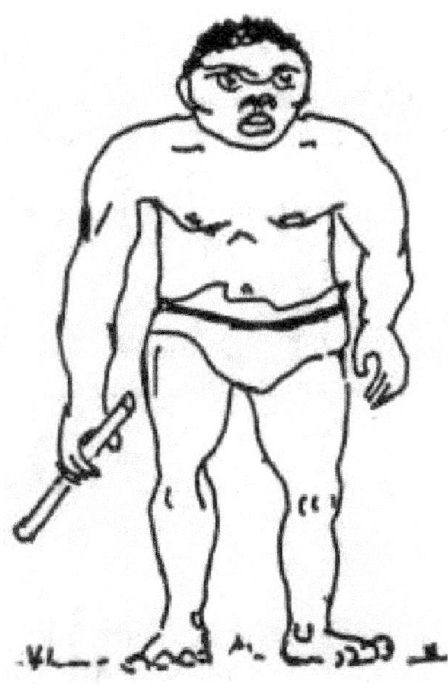

"Kara-Komba"or Bush Dwarf,
  after native description (Christian le Noël)

Why have these hominians escaped a thorough study until now ? Doubtless because, having been the subjects of game beats for thousands of years by black *Homo sapiens*, they have become suspicious and rare. Their very reproduction has doubtless become difficult due to the conditions of their precarious and furtive lifestyle; perhaps they have even become completely nocturnal. Their nomadic existence in such a vast country does not favour observation.

In the bush, certain hamlets of present day tribes are totally unknown; during the 1969 cholera epidemic in Chad, the authorities discovered tribes which had escaped all control by the administration for years, living in inaccessible zones. It required this exceptional epidemic for military helicopters checking out these regions at the end of the vaccination program to discover these unknown sedentary population, i.e. it is relatively easy for small human groups to pass unnoticed, especially if they are deliberately hiding.

Neither animals, nor men in the modern sense of the term, what then can these unknown hominians be? A deeply interesting enigma to elucidate at the dawn of the 21st century, where all the mysteries of our origins are far from being entirely explained.

References:

(1) ROUMEGUERE-EBERHARDT, Jacqueline 1984 - Enquêtes Récentes sur des Hominoïdes Inconnus en Afrique Orientale. *Communication faite pour le 3ème Congrès de l'ISC*, Université de Paris VI (Jussieu), Juin. [Recent enquiries on unknown hominoids in East Africa. *Communication made for the 3rd Congress of the ISC*, University of Paris VI (Jussieu), June]

(2) ROUMEGUERE-EBERHARDT, Jacqueline 1990 - *Dossier X - Les Hominidés non identifiés d'Afrique.*[X-File - The unidentified hominids of Africa] Paris, Robert Laffont

(3) ANONYMOUS,1979 - Monsieur X, Ape-Man - *Fate*, vol. **32** : 23-26 (July).

. . . .

Astute readers will note that this thesis is based on evidence and opinions which vary considerably in both reliability and relevance. So, rather than write a long dissertation myself, I shall leave its analysis to my readers, and limit myself to a few background comments.

True pygmies are, by definition, no more than 150 cm (4 ft 11 in) in height, and frequently shorter. At the present time, they are all restricted to the dense rainforest, or nearby, those of the Central African Republic being limited to the southwest corner. However, it is likely that, in the past, before the expansion of agricultural tribes, that extended farther out, into the savanna. About 2450 BC, Harkhuf, the viceroy of Pharaoh Pepi II, ventured far south and returned with a captive pygmy. In Book II of his *Histories*, the 5th century BC writer, Herodotus recounted the story of a group of Libyans who crossed the desert, and were captured by a race of black dwarfs who took them though a vast tract of marshy country (? the Sudd) to their town on the banks of a crocodile-infested river which flowed west to east (? the Bahr el Ghazal).

The Khoisan - the Bushmen and Hottentots of southern Africa - are not much taller than the pygmies. They are known to have been displaced by southwardly moving pastoral Bantu in historical times.

Homo habilis and *Homo erectus* were of more normal human stature. As pre-human species, they almost certainly were more hirsute than *Homo sapiens*, which did not lose its body hair until about 1.2 million years ago.

All short races in the tropics are of slight build. There are no known heavy set, very strong pygmies.

The footprints measured by the author at 15 to 18 cm are consistent with a height of 3 ft 4 in to 4 feet. A stride of 50 cm is consistent with the latter height. If Oumar Boukar's estimate of 1.10 metres (3 ft 7 in) for the height of the individual he encountered is accurate, and was accurately recorded, the bush dwarf was very small indeed. However, it must be remembered that there is no reason the individual, or the footprints, represented the tallest person in the community. Indeed, the tallest members are always in a minority. In 1990 I stayed in an Mbuti pygmy village, and although the adult men would not have been more than 4 ft 9 in (they came up to my armpit, and I am a 6 footer), I can assure you the women and teenage boys were really, really small.

Finally, anything which carries an axe, and wears sandals and a pubic apron, is a human being - who presumably knows how to make fire, and shelter for the night. Human hunter gatherers are semi-nomadic, remaining in the same encampment for weeks or months at a time. By both necessity and instinct, they live in social groups - two or three families at a minimum during periods when food is dispersed, and coalescing into aggregations of scores, or even hundreds, during times of plenty. The idea of a race of pygmies living in the open woodlands, without their camping sites ever being discovered by the outside world, and without making any attempt to contact the outsiders, even to satisfy their curiosity, has a very low plausibility rating.

Just the same, there are still the footprints, and the witnesses . . .

Chapter 11

Tales from the Kenyan Woods

In the previous chapter we saw mention of Jacqueline Roumeguère-Eberhardt (1927 - 2006). She was a cultural anthropologist with a rather colourful personal life. Born in South Africa, where she conducted anthropological studies on the native tribes, she took French nationality when she married a French diplomat in 1957. However, after moving to Kenya, she left him for her Maasai assistant, who was both illiterate and a polygamist, but they apparently got on extremely well.

Her studies on African anthropology were extensive, but she caused controversy in 1984 with the publication of *Dossier X: les hominidés non-identifiés des forêts d'Afrique* ("X File: the unidentified hominids of the African forests"). I can't say I have read it and, in any case, it would be too long to translate. However, I can copy a report of a press conference she gave on Tuesday 3 October 1978, which was printed in a number of Australian newspapers in the next two days, and no doubt in many other newspapers in other countries. My thanks go to Dr. Ralph Molnar, who provided me with copies of *The Queensland Times* of 4 October 1978, page 23 and the *Northern Territory News* of 5 October, page 16. Except for the headlines, they are identical.

Personally, I find extraordinary the claim that there is not a single mystery species, but four, and that they are light skinned. I also find the reference to a bow and poison arrows remarkable, because these are instruments of a sophisticated society. (The Australian Aborigines, for example, did not possess them.) It might be noted that, although the Nandi and Mau forests of western Kenya are quite extensive, they have nevertheless been fully explored.

Just the same, she was an accomplished anthropologist, fluent in many African languages, and with a long-time rapport with the local people, and she must have got her information from somewhere. So let us look at what she had to say.

. . . .

NAIROBI. - Hominids - man-like creatures half way between *Homo sapiens* and his simian ancestors - are in Kenya's forests, according to a French Anthropologist here.

Jacqueline Roumeguère-Eberhardt of the French National Scientific Research Centre appealed at a press conference here for a systematic study of the shy creatures.

She said that since 1966, when she began studying Nilotic and Hamitic tribes such as the Masai and Samburu, she had noted 33 reported meetings between hominids and Kenyan tribesmen. Mrs. Roumeguère-Eberhardt said she had interviewed 17 eyewitnesses and had collected several objects that once belonged to hominids.

The encounters with humans went back 60 years and involved four types of hominid, of both sexes, she went on. With the exception of one type of pygmy-like stature, all were tall, light-skinned with colouring ranging from grey to beige, sometimes covered with fur or with long hair, she said.

According to Mrs. Roumeguère-Eberhardt, the creatures had been seen on several occasions using clubs to kill large animals such as water buffalo[36].They would then eat some of the organs, particularly the liver, or carry away parts of the prey, she said.

She added that one of the four recorded species appeared to have evolved more than the others. He was the only one to have clothing - a worn animals skin - and to have been armed with anything more sophisticated than a club. She showed journalists a bow and poison-tipped arrows which she said were of a kind never seen before in Kenya.

Mrs. Roumeguère-Eberhardt declined to say exactly were the hominids could be found, fearing that they might become completely extinct if their last hiding places were known. She said reported sightings had become less frequent in the last few decades.

---

[36] I presume the journalist mistook a reference to the African buffalo, which does not frequent the water, and is *very dangerous* - even for someone with a spear, rather than a club.

Chapter 12

Two Unknown Bipedal Apes in the Congo

Charles Cordier(1897-1994) was a Swiss zoo collector who worked for the Bronx Zoo in New York. In the late 1940s he and his wife, Emy made a lengthy expedition to the Belgian Congo (now the Democratic Republic of the Congo), specifically to collect the Congo peacock, which had been identified only in 1936! However, what I presume was his last expedition to the Congo coincided with the violence and anarchy of Congo Independence. Nevertheless, as well as catching gorillas using nets (they don't do that sort of thing any more) in what can only be labelled the geographic centre of Africa, he heard rumours of not one, but two unknown apes. At least this area of dense tropical rainforest is one place where such species could exist, unknown to the rest of the world. Here, then, is his account, translated from the French.

....

Charles Cordier (1963), "Deux anthropoïdes inconnus marchant debout au Congo ex-Belge", (Two unknown anthropoids walking upright in the former Belgian Congo.) *Genus* 19:175-182

This is not a sensational report, nor is it concrete proof of their existence, but the collected indices are so numerous and troubling that, for me, their existence is beyond the shadow of doubt.

I was in the Congo from November 1947 to June 1949 in order to capture animals for the Bronx Zoo, New York and from April 1956 to December 1961 to collect live animals for a film and, later, on my own account.

It was only in January 1960 that the natives mentioned the names of these two anthropoids before me or, to be more exact, I started to get interested in following up revelations made by them on the subject of the existence of an aquatic mammal which appeared to be a dwarf dugong.

At the end of June 1960 the Congolese independence supervened, along with its sequel of troubles. I was able to make investigations during the first six months of 1960 in the environs of our camp in the Walikale Forest, situated at 750 metres [2460 ft] of altitude in the province of Kivu. I made a tour by automobile commencing at Walikale and followed a section of the road leading to Stanleyville[37] up to 20 km [12½ miles] beyond the Osso River. At this point there is a mining road which makes a bend towards the rear on the left and along the right bank of the Lowa River, which I crossed by ferry to beyond Pense Misale. On this section is found Socomukanga.

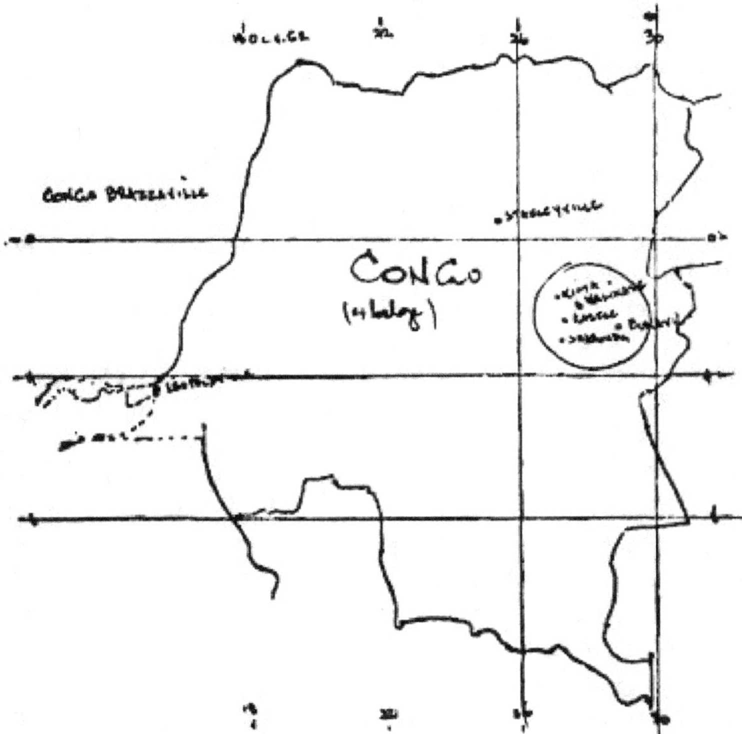

By the testimonies collected later and farther away, I had to pass "to the final riddle" [uncertain colloquialism] this region, when I had crossed it in haste, questioning the natives very little. After having crossed the Lowa, I wanted to go up the left bank of this river, to ferry across the Uku River in order to head down in a southerly direction towards the mining centre of Kasese. I was then able to follow this itinerary, I crossed the epicentre of these ape-men, in the light of information subsequently received. Alas, a ferry or bridge was out of service on this section, and I had to resign myself to taking another road leading to

---

Kima. This mining centre has a hospital which, from time to time, receive inhabitants injured by the mountain gorillas which, at this spot, come down to an altitude of 500 metres [1640 feet]. This is also one of the extreme western points in their distribution. From Kima a road goes to Punia, and one can join Kasese from the south through a landscape overturned and devastated by the mining operations.

After only a score of kilometres, the landscape once more became rough and timbered. I halted in order to photograph a beautiful clump of raffia palms when up came several natives, to whom I posed some questions on the subject of the ape-men. These people then set out to frighten and insult my two native travelling companions in order to indulge themselves in making investigations for a white man on the subject of the "forest devils", as one of them called them in French. After this encounter my two employees were rather crestfallen and depressed. Nevertheless, 15 km [9 miles] to the south of Kasese, on the main road leading to the Lugulu River, and the headquarters of the Shabunda territory, we halted in a little village, where a religious service was under way. Our intention was to ask permission to pass the night there. After prayers and songs, I mentioned the "Kakundakari", and then a young woman suckling a child said, as if it were the most natural statement in the world: "I saw one which was living in a cage at Sokomukange in January 1957. It had been found dead, or almost so, in a snare of steel wire. The hunter brought it to the village, the being recovered, they confined it, and it afterwards escaped. Hundreds of blacks and dozens of whites went to see it." A young man who was present confirmed the accuracy of the account.

After that, my two travelling companions had recovered from their depression and the next day we continued, full of expectations, towards the south. Alas, the more we sought information near the rare inhabitants we encountered, the more evasive became their answers. At the Lugulu River, which marks the limit of the distribution of the gorilla towards the south, the name of Kakundakari was no longer current, and people talked about the enigmatic "Niaka-Ambúguzá", whose tracks, like the footprints of a child, they often found along the water.

We pushed our enquiry up to Lukavia and Shabunda, and we took the road which led to Bukavu. Despite lack of success everywhere, nevertheless in a village close to Ikozi, where the people had been catching antelopes in the environs for months, a woman, without presenting herself, let us know that she had seen a young ape-man alive in Sokomukanga, and when we were engaged in the mountain defile called Kimbili, a man told us all about a memorable hunt he had taken part in close to Walikale, a long way to the north. During this hunt, a little ape-man charged into a net, and immediately disappeared. Precisely a few weeks before, I had paid a visit to the owner of the hunting net which the "Kakundakari" had momentarily invaded.

Two very old men living close to our former forest camp at Walikale had seen a Kakundakari killed 40 to 45 years ago. One of the witnesses claimed that the head resembled that of a human infant, whereas the other categorically affirmed that the head was that of an ape.

From August to November 1961, I twice captured, in the region of Walike, entire bands of gorillas, aided by Mr. Paul Leloup[38], a herpetologist who was familiar with the Congo for a long time. We then collected as much information as possible on the two anthropoids, but we did not dare to make a journey of inspection which would have led us towards Kasese and the region immediately to the north, and of which I have just spoken, because of the lamentable state of the roads ruined by exceptional rains and the evident incapacity of the administration to provide maintenance or repairs. We would have perhaps arrived at the destination, but we would not have been able to return because of a bridge carried away by the waters, or a band of indisciplined soldiers would have been able to take the fuel or even the vehicle . . .

We had the luck to depart the Congo with eight living gorillas, but we had no wish to retrace our steps, as certain authorities were becoming very xenophobic and irrational.

But enough introductions ... and here are some stipulations: these two anthropoids, certainly very, very rare, are beings which inspire terror, and the generality of mortals in the Congo say that they are spirits or ghosts: "Mushumbi or Gitáni", but admit that in this case the words mean rare or almost never seen.

Just to see them is alleged to make one sick, and to draw their presence to the attention of white men would result in the worst consequences. The little anthropoid to which I give the name *Congopithecus* is alleged to reach a height of 2 to 3 feet [60 to 90 cm]. The hairs on its head are stiff and form a kind of mane down its neck. Its colour is black. The body its covered with short, sparse hair. An informant who claimed to me to have killed one which was wrestling his

---

[38] Paul the Wolf!

wife, who had gone alone far from the village to fish for crabs, stipulated that the belly is whitish and strongly resembles that of the brush-tailed porcupine, or *Atherurus*. This subject, transfixed by a spear, took hours to die, not ceasing to kick around until the villagers threw some boiling water on it, according to what this informant said.

In the region of Walkale *Congopithecus* is called "Kakundakari" by the Bakano and Bakondjo, towards the north the Bakumu people call it "Amajúngi", to the south among the Warega it is the "Niaka Ambúguzá" and to the east among the Batembo "Ambátcha". Mr. Leloup told me that on the left bank of the Lomami River in Orientale Province, the natives talk about the "Lisisíngo".

It moves on the ground erect, quite frequently its tracks are parallel to those of a herd of bushpigs (*Potamochoerus*), it fishes for crabs in the small streams by moving away the stones, steals the game out of traps and empties the traps for fish and crabs, appears to be almost exclusively carnivorous, but does not disdain the scarlet fruit of the ginger locally known as "Matungulu".

Just before nightfall it retires into a cave or an empty tree trunk where it piles up wood as if it wanted to make a fire, which it doesn't know how. Numbers of one to three are encountered. If it discovers a fish net, it amuses itself by sticking a finger into each space as if to count them.

Despite its small size it appears to possess immense strength, capable of carrying off, or dragging away, a 14 year old child. One informant described having once found a little one, entirely white, on a bed of grass on the sandy bank of a small river. He ran to the village to advise the elders, but the little one had disappeared by the time he returned.

On the road from Walikale leading to Masisi I visited, at the 2 km mark, a cave alleged to have been inhabited in all weathers by the Kakundakaris.

A shooting range and the fields having been established in the proximity, the Kakundakari only goes there occasionally. I myself saw there the signs of a slide on the edge towards the interior of the cave lower down, terminating with a footprint resembling that of a child. It was 12 cm [4.7 in] long, the thumb [big toe] proportionally longer than for a human being, and the fingers numbering four, the little finger being atrophied, according to what certain people said.[39]

At the back of the cave, too low for human beings, there were the ends of dead timber and sections of a termite mound placed there by someone. Whether these signs were genuine, or a hoax, I cannot say.

The big anthropoid or spirit, to which I give the name *Paranthropus congensis* is alleged to be vegetarian. It is a being with black hair, those of its head being long and dense, covering the head and hiding its face when it bends down. It is as big as a man or bigger, with very broad shoulders, always walks upright, and often has a piece of wood in its hand. It climbs trees to collect honey from the bee hives. It drops down from the heights if surprised. It eats the méke-méké or itenangwa tubers which grow in the wet parts of the forest. It likes ginger fruit. It demolishes the dead tree trunks in order to remove the larvae. It howls, especially at night, in a more frightening manner than a gorilla, but certain people say that this is the cry of the water chevrotain. Indistinct in the forest, following the crests, most informants say that it does not shelter in caves.

Among the Bakano and Bakondjo people it is called "Kikomba", among the Bakumu, "Apamándi or Abanaánji". The Warrega call it "Zuluzúgu" and the Batembo "Tshingómbe."

It is a being reputed to have immense strength, apt to charge at a man simply to wrestle with him or rain blows of a club on him, for it often have the end of a branch or the handle of axe loose in its hand. The sole defence is to play dead. It then goes away in order to look for something to cover the victim's body. That is the moment for the unlucky human to make himself scarce.

In the neighbourhood of Obaye, in the territory of Walikale, a man is alleged to live with a useless arm as the result of a fight with a Kikomba.

In making the investigations of the Kakundakari cave near Walikale, a man presented himself who is supported to have been pursued by a Kikomba in January 1960 at Km. 14 [8.7 mile] of the mining road leading to the gold mine of Umate. I was able to persuade him to get into my vehicle in order to show me the site. After a run of 60 km. [37 m] we arrived at the exact spot. We ascertained that the vegetation at the side of the road had just been crushed by the step of a man leaving at a right

---

[39] This is clearly an ape footprint, consistent with a height of 79 cm or 31 inches, assuming its build was proportional to a human being's.

angle to the road towards the interior. At the beginning, a gutter made the impression of a path. After having followed the tracks about a dozen metres, there were no more signs of an advance. We turned back and saw that the being had rejoined the road by a small detour. At the end of several metres following the edge of the road, in a small, flat space covered with fine sand, there was a most impressive plantar footprint. Superficially, it resembled a man's, but it was only 20 cm [8 in] long and very broad. It was also peculiar in that the second digit was much longer than the big toe. A quick investigation permitted us to ascertain that, farther on, the presumed "Kikomba" had regained the trail which crossed the road obliquely at this point.

In making preparations to photograph this footprint, a formidable storm intervened, and the sole tangible proof was effaced . ..

The proofs and indications concerning the Kikomba are much less than those collected on the subject of the Kakundakari. But I have still to mention that the section of road Walikale-Osso River, a year previously and accompanied by a score of men, we took information on the subject of a savanna or swamp in the forest called "Ido or Idambo" frequented by bongo antelopes which we were seeking, the men of the site related to my men, such that I could not doubt it, that in establishing a hunting camp at the edge of this "Ido", the occupants of the shelter were invariably disturbed at night time by the bad tricks of the kikomba which, during the night would come and tear away the leaves of the roofs and shake the huts. They cited to my men the case of an itinerant trader pursued close to the main road by a Kikomba. In order to save himself, the man threw away his backpack and threw himself into a canoe lying on the bank. The frustrated Kikomba picked up the backpack, opened it, and scattered the contents.

One is entitled to wonder if the "abominable forest man", the Kikomba or Apamándi is perhaps not the male of the little Kakundakári? It is really regrettable that I could not get information on the subject in earlier years, for it seems they are found in all the unpopulated forests of the central Congo basin where I had travelled a lot in search of the Congo peacock and the bongo antelope. When I questioned the men why they had never spoken to me about it, they replied simply: "You never asked us."

To those who doubt, or claim to invalidate my revelations on the basis that this region has been prospected and passed through in every direction and that nothing unknown could be hidden there, I reply that the region is an veritable geographic nightmare, extremely difficult to traverse, and that the prospectors are always accompanied by a large number of men who, convinced of the existence of these beings, advance with the loudest noise possible in order to cause them to flee.

· · · ·· ·· · ··

Needless to say, the scientific names he coined for them are not valid, because no type specimens are provided. Nevertheless, from the descriptions, they are clearly apes, but what kind? Unlike most of the higher primates, but like most of the bigfoot-type species reported around the world, they are essentially solitary. I therefore doubt his speculation that they represent different sexes of the same species. When the male of a species is twice the size of the female, it is usually because he keeps a harem.

The author is, of course, correct in his last paragraph. That jungle could hide anything. Let us not forget that it has been only in this current century that the Bili apes were discovered, while Further east we have the koolookamba which, as I explained earlier, is probably an undescribed third species of chimpanzee. You probably imagine that chimpanzees are spread out over the whole of the jungle. Think again! Cordier didn't mention them in his article. However, Dr Geza Teleki and the Committee for Conservation and Care of Chimpanzees produced a map containing a number of small black blotches indicating known areas, surrounded by heavy stippling for "probable areas", plus a broad stretch of fine stippling, covering most of the forest, for "possible areas". If we know so little about the distribution of our closest relative, which lives in sizeable bands, what else can be out there?

INDEX

Other Books by the Author

The following books are all in print, and available from Amazon.

Bunyips and Bigfoots. up-dated second edition. The classic survey of Australia's mystery animals: bunyips, sea serpents, the North Queensland tiger, Tasmanian tigers on the mainland, pumas and black panthers, yowies, and others - all fully documented. Originally published in 1996, it was republished and up-dated in 2021.

The Stranger from the Stars. A science fiction novel about a group of hikers who rescue an injured alien from a crashed flying saucer. Having followed the UFO scene for more than 50 years, I have ensured that the story is "realistic", in that all the phenomena described have been reported many times in the literature.

The Truth About Bunyips. Every Australian has heard about bunyips, but no-one knows what they are supposed to look like. Based on a huge number of recently digitalised old documents and newspapers, this short book should be the definitive work on the subject.

Australian Sea Serpents. Sea serpents really exist, and have been visiting Australian shores for a long time. I have now trawled through dozens to digitalised newspapers to produce what I expect will also become the definitive work on the subject. More than half of the case histories are new - that is to say, they have never been published in book form by other researchers.

Forgotten Sea Serpents. This is an adjunct to the above: a large collection of reports of sea serpents outside of Australia which have, apparently, been missed by other researchers. The book should be welcomed by cryptozoologists looking to complete their documentation on the subject.

Savages and Saints by Leon and Theophila Philippi - but ghost written by yours truly. This is the story of my parents-in-law: a farm boy from Nebraska, and a pastor's daughter from the Eyre Peninsula of South Australia, who were thrown together under unusual circumstances, married after a whirlwind courtship, and set out for New Guinea as missionaries. The sort of experiences they went through are beyond the imagination of the present generation.

Trials of a Tourist. I've been an international tourist for most of my adult life, visiting remote places even millionaires haven't seen. So now I have written a humorous account of the quirky things I have experienced, as well as the "plot against tourists", by which the world conspires to make travelling as inconvenient as possible.

The Gospels: Harmonized and Annotated (two volumes): Here I present the four gospels together in chronological order, with parallel texts side by side, and with a discussion of the situation in first century Israel in which they were embedded.

Apparitions: tulpas, ghosts, fairies, and even stranger things. This is not an ordinary book on ghosts, but coves a whole range of paranormal apparitions: tulpas and other creations of the mind, ghosts, fairies, and things which are more bizarre - but all fully documented.

A Zoologist Looks at Science Fiction. H. G. Wells said that the essence of science fiction was the suspension of disbelief. As a zoologist, I have a bit more difficulty than most. In this short book I examine the mistakes made by science fiction writers in their creations of monsters and aliens, not to mention robots.

The Repat Racket. An insider's report on Veterans' Affairs. Originally published in 2010, and now republished, it reveals the way in which good intentions for compensating ex-servicemen resulted in a grotesque legal system open to enormous abuses.